EBRAHIM GOLESTAN

An Encounter with Dylan Thomas

برخوردها
در
زمانهٔ برخورد

Edited *&* Translated by
Abbas Milani

MAGE PUBLISHERS

This book is part of a series of Iranian Studies publications made possible by the Hamid and Christina Moghadam Program in Iranian Studies at Stanford University.

Copyright © 2022 Mage Publishers
Cover tile: Iranian fifteenth-century glazed tile. Photo Credit: © RMN-Grand Palais / Art Resource, NY.

Calligraphy on page 31: Amir-Sadeq Tehrani

Mage Publishers Inc.
www.mage.com

Library of Congress Cataloging-in-Publication Data
Available at the Library of Congress

First hardcover edition
ISBN: 978-1-949445-41-1

Visit Mage online: www.mage.com
eMail: as@mage.com

CONTENTS

For Bita Daryabari
&
Shidan and Mehran Taslimi
In appreciation of their passion for Persian Art

THE CENTENNIAL OF EBRAHIM GOLESTAN

Abbas Milani

At the age of a hundred, Ebrahim Golestan remains, as he has been for much of his adult life, a towering figure in modern Iranian arts and literature. He also remains in exile, as he has been for most of his adult life.

Even when he still lived in Iran, Golestan wrote of feeling like an exile. In his "Encounter with Dylan Thomas," translated here, (pp. 31–113) he begins with a description of this virtual self-imposed exile—of a room "far away from the city … away from its smells and smoke, and from its sounds and its hustle and bustle" (p. 33).[1] Here, then, was his intellectual home; what he called his actual home "happened to be elsewhere" (p. 33).

All his life, Golestan has lived in this state of psychological as well as physical exile. "Exile," he wrote. "had taken place even when I lived in Tehran."[2] Yet he identifies very strongly with Iranian culture. "Iran," he has often said, "is not just a

---

1. All page numbers after a quotation refer to pages in the present volume.
2. Ebrahim Golestan, *Nameh be Simin* [Letter to Simin], with an introduction by Abbas Milani, (Tehran: BaztabNegar, 1399/2021), p. 34.

geographical unit; it is a cultural state." Golestan believes that Iran as a cultural state "is as powerful and expansive as the culture that thrives inside [him]."[3] Indeed, "cultures are not static ... the realm of a culture is never [confined to] a small corner of earth, or a dot on a map." Referring to how an imaginary Republic of Letters promotes "active relations between vital intellects," he goes on to define culture as "the constant and dynamic" exploration of ideas.[4] More than anything, in other words, he regards himself as a citizen of that republic.

Not surprisingly, then, in his conversation with Dylan Thomas that took place in 1951 we see poignant examples of his sense of exile. The text was written some fifty years ago and published recently when he was ninety eight.[5] There he quotes one of his favorite couplets from the innumerous lines of Persian poetry he knows by heart: "Without a hundred thousand people, solitude; / With a hundred thousand people, solitude" (p. 83).

Fortunately for us, this psychological and physical exile in Golestan has not begot his silence, or intellectual apathy. His motto in life of being true to one's calling and one's beliefs comes from another of his favorite couplets in Persian poetry—one he also happened to recite for Thomas: "Like a mountain endure, like a lilac laugh, / Like a wheel whirl, and like a cloud drizzle" (p. 83). Iranian culture and literature have for almost a century been the increasingly appreciative recipients of his productive bounty.

Neither his own enduring philosophy nor profuse praise or appreciation by others, have given Golestan an exaggerated sense of his own importance (a common trait in many exiles). He

---

3. Ebrahim Golestan, *Gofteha* [an anthology of his essays, short stories and interviews, covering four decades] (New Jersey: Rowzan, 1994), p. 51.

4. Ibid., p. 51.

5. Ebrahim Golestan, *Barkhordha dar Zaman Barkhord* [Encounters in the Season of Encounter], (Tehran, BaztabNegar, 1400/2021).

maintains a sense of distance even when writing about his own work, admitting that, rather than being exceptional, he is simply a "normal man of normal height and average intelligence … in an avenue of dwarfs":

> You wanted to see correctly; maybe you didn't see correctly, but you saw honestly … You knew that your attempts to see correctly, and consequently describe correctly, made you a stranger. It made you different and in your own mind it made you proud of yourself. Such pride was rueful; it was a pride that came as a result of the dwarfish nature of your surroundings; the surroundings were short; you were not tall.[6]

This self-critical view of himself and his time must be assessed in the context of the pride Golestan takes in Iran's rich cultural heritage. His lament is not based on self-loathing or Iran-bashing—but a call to fellow Iranians to become better custodians and critics of Iran's rich but complicated past.

It is because of his continual creativity and persistent cultural critiques, as well as a deep-seated aversion to intellectual shibboleths and received opinions that his books are still read and praised, his films are viewed and acclaimed both at home and abroad,[7] and his singularity as a high-profile intellectual and artist more appreciated than ever before. The purpose of this slender volume is to commemorate his centennial. It is in no way intended as a critical overview of his life and work but only a small token in celebration of a life marked by endless curiosity,

---

6. Ibid, pp. 22–3.
7. The Fondazione Cineteca di Bologna, an internationally celebrated archive for preserving and restoring some of cinema's great masterpieces, has already restored Golestan's *A Fire* (1961), *The Hills of Marlik* (1963), *Brick and Mirror* (1965), *The Crown Jewels of Iran* (1966) and *The Harvest and the Seed* (1965), and is working on restoring several others, including *Mysteries of the Ghost Valley* (1974).

ceaseless creativity, and aesthetic acumen—a life devoted to exposing, in sometimes sobering frankness, the empty bombast of popular dogmas.

I first met Ebrahim Golestan in September 1999 to ask him about one instance of his speaking truth to power. In spite of his reputation for candor, I could still scarcely believe that the story I had heard could be true. At the time, I was working on a book on the life of the Iranian politician Amir Abbas Hoveyda (1919–79). He had served as prime minister during the reign of the Shah for more than thirteen years, and after the Iranian Revolution was sentenced to death by a kangaroo court.[8] Hoveyda's brother, Fereydoun Hoveyda, a prominent Iranian writer, film critic, and diplomat and a close friend of Golestan, had told me that, one night at Fereydoun's house, Golestan had a tense confrontation with the then prime minister. At that point, Golestan already had become a near-mythic presence in my mind. I had used his fiction as a study text in the early 1970s when I was working as a teaching assistant at Berkeley. In the 1990s, I had heard much about his personal traits from another of his close friends, the writer Sadeq Chubak (1916–98). And yet, the story Fereydoun recounted still sounded fantastical.

According to Fereydoun, on the night Golestan came to visit him, the prime minister was unexpectedly there too. Golestan had known Amir Abbas Hoveyda for many years, even before the mid-fifties when they both worked at the Iranian Oil Company. As Hoveyda ascended the political ladder, Golestan subjected him to increasingly harsh criticism. One of Golestan's novellas, "Tales from Bygone Times," for instance, includes a character "whose accent was mixed, whose intelligence was fine, and whose jokes were from notes. He used a cane for no reason and lusted for power and status despite claiming to have no desire for either."

---

8. For an account of his life and death, see Abbas Milani, *The Persian Sphinx: Amir Abbas Hoveyda and the Riddle of the Iranian Revolution* (Washington, D.C.: Mage, 2000).

If these details were not enough to reveal to every literate Iranian that the character was obviously a thinly disguised allusion to Hoveyda, Golestan ended the description by saying "all of this was obviously visible"—a pun on the name Hoveyda, which in Persian means "visible."[9] Hoveyda is subjected to even greater criticism, at times bordering on derision, in Golestan's production of *Don Juan in Hell*—based on his translation of the third act of George Bernard Shaw's *Man and Superman*—and in his film *Mysteries of the Ghost Valley*. When Golestan unexpectedly encountered Hoveyda at Fereydoun's house, *Mysteries of the Ghost Valley,* released in 1974, had already been banned after only a few days of screening. Golestan believed Hoveyda to be complicit in the decision to ban the film. The real surprise in the Procrustean atmosphere of censorship at the time was that the film ever received a license to be shown as it so clearly made fun of the Shah, Hoveyda, and many of the ruling elite. More than once Golestan has declared that he did not intend to parody the Shah or any other individual. It is, however, impossible to watch the film and not see the Shah as a direct focus of the poignant parody. It was an indication of Golestan's ability to use his standing and the rivalry between different bureaucracies—in this case, the Ministry of Culture and Iran's Radio and Television Organization—to get the film's screening license without any previewing by censors. As soon as the film was screened, however, and the audiences began to jeer and clap at just the right moments, SAVAK (Organization of National Security and Information)—the powerful secret police and intelligence service—realized that the film was a parody of the Shah and his regime and was predicting an imminent revolution. SAVAK therefore ordered it to be banned. At the time of the chance

---

9. Ebrahim Golestan, "Az ruzgar-e raft-e hekayat," [Tales from Bygone Times], in *Mad o meh* [High Tide and the Fog] (Tehran: Mihan Publishers, 1969), p. 65.

meeting in Fereydoun's house, Golestan believed—as he still does—that Hoveyda was the chief mastermind behind the ban.

According to Fereydoun, when Golestan arrived at his house the prime minister made a comment which Golestan interpreted as a snide remark about his attire. What began as "jocular verbal banter" soon turned into a more serious confrontation. Golestan, angered, took off his shirt, crumpled it into a ball and threw it at the prime minister, insisting that he should "smell it, [as] it has the sweet smell of conscience ... not the stench of someone who has sold his soul."[10] To his credit, Amir Abbas called off his security detail and responded by offering Golestan a glass of special French wine, a recent gift the French ambassador had sent the prime minister.

Although I had no reason to doubt Fereydoun's honesty in telling me the story, I still needed to confirm the details with Golestan—and, more importantly, ask about his views on Amir Abbas Hoveyda. He kindly answered all my questions and confirmed the details of the encounter. Thus began a friendship that has lasted until today. Through it all, I have seen him lead a life dedicated to art, contemplation, beauty, and speaking truth to power, combined with an infinite kindness to friends. When, a few years after meeting him, I wrote a book on the Shah[11], he generously read the entire manuscript and offered copious marginal notes, rich in detail, astute in observation, and always frank in tone. At one hundred years of age, he is as relentlessly dedicated to these same principles as he was in his salad days.

Golestan is as likely to obsess about the perfect placement of a vase of flowers on a mantel in his bedroom as he is about a comma in his pristine, precise, and invariably poetic prose. I have witnessed, in awe, how—even as he neared his centennial—he diligently started a new essay on another former prime minister, Mohammad Mosaddegh (1882–1967)—a man he had met on

---

10. Milani, *The Persian Sphinx*, p. 260.
11. Abbas Milani, *The Shah*, (New York: Palgrave, 2010).

numerous occasions, and whose trial following his fall in August 1953 Golestan covered as a photo-journalist. In fact, virtually all the most iconic images of that historic trial are Golestan's work.[12]

As Golestan worked on his essay on Mosaddegh, he also spent endless hours in meticulously correcting galleys for two of his memoirs—*Encounters in the Season of Encounter* and *Mokhtar in His Time*[13]. *Encounters* is a detailed account of two important encounters Golestan had in 1951, at the tumultuous time of Iran's decision to nationalize its oil. The first meeting was with Dylan Thomas (1914–53), the Welsh poet who had been sent to Iran to make a film.[14] The second was with the committee sent by Mosaddegh, as the prime minister, to the city of Abadan to take over the oil refinery from the departing British. Golestan's sympathies were—and still are—clearly with Mosaddegh, yet he realized the committee he had dispatched to take over the industry were as clueless about the complexity of the task at hand as Thomas was about making a film about Iran's oil industry.

Mokhtar in His Time is a brilliant essay-cum-memoir about Amir-Mokhtar Karimpour Shirazi (1921–54), known simply as Mohktar—an often overlooked political character, derided and disbelieved by the left, despised and distrusted by the right, and used by some to attack the Shah and his regime. Although Mohktar was a member of the working class, the "comrades" in the Tudeh Party who claimed to represent the proletariat viewed him with nothing but disdain and distrust—all save Ebrahim

---

12. For a sample of some of those photos and a discussion with Golestan about how he was granted access to the court to take those photos, see "Interview with Golestan," *40 Cheragh*, 786, May 25, 2020.

13. Ebrahim Golestan, *Mokhtar Dar Zaman* [Mokhtar in His Time], (Tehran, Baztabnegar, 1402/2022).

14. For a discussion of an account of that journey according to Thomas, see "Their Man in Abadan: Dylan Thomas in Iran" (pp. 115–35).

and Fakhri Golestan, Golestan's independent and remarkably erudite wife. Along with Golestan's *Letter to Simin,*[15] *Mokhtar in His Time* and *Encounters in the Season of Encounter* form a brilliant triptych that offers a searing and scathing, but always informed and informative, panorama of Iran's intellectual and political history in the second half of the twentieth century. The books complement Golestan's major feature films *Mysteries of the Ghost Valley* and *Brick and Mirror*. In each book or film, one aspect of Iran's mangled modernity and the tragedy that awaits it beyond the horizon are mapped out. The three books together, in terms of their breadth of vision, carefully drawn portraits, and participant-observer view of modern history, are akin to André Malraux's *Antimémoires* (1967)—often praised as a masterpiece of a new kind of memoir. In each case, the text is shaped by the narrative flair and astute observational powers of a polished novelist and informed by the rigor and local knowledge of an erudite historian and aesthete.

Even those who have often jealously dismissed Golestan—on account of his artistic success, his affluence, his storied love affair with the poet Forough Farrokhzad, his "castle" in England, or his unabashed frankness in offering critical views of those he deemed to be peddlers of kitsch—have never been able to ignore him. To the cultural paparazzi, his private life, particularly every detail of his love affair with Forough Farrokhzad, has been an incessant subject of sometimes prurient curiosity. By contrast, his fascinating and continued admiration for his first wife, Fakhri, and his quiet enduring love of Ashi Esfandiari, a woman he met in 1971 and who has been his constant companion for much of the last half-century, have received little attention. The result of his marriage to Fakhri was two children—Lili, who is now a successful translator and gallery owner in Iran, and Kaveh,

---

15. Ebrahim Golestan, *Nameh be Simin* [Letter to Simin], (Tehran, Baztabnegar, 1389/2010).

who established his reputation as one of Iran's most successful photo-journalists.

In 2003, tragedy struck the family when Kaveh, on assignment in Iraq, was killed by a land mine. Golestan has suffered grief in stoic silence. In talking about his son's death, he has more than once remarked that his only solace is that Kaveh had at least realized his potential as an artist and left behind an impressive body of work.[16] Virtually each time he talks about Forough, or Kaveh, tears well up in his eyes and, more often than not, his voice breaks. No discussion of Fakhri is also ever without Golestan's profuse praise for her brilliance, her endless love of her children, and his own continued love and admiration for her.

Ebrahim Golestan was born on October 18, 1922 in the city of Shiraz. Though he has lived only a small portion of his life there, he not only retains some of his Shirazi dialect, but has a contagious passion for what he believes to be the city's singular excellence in almost everything—from its cuisine and mountains to its poets and historic buildings. His parents both came from the city's prominent families.

His mother, Fatemeh, was keenly interested in getting an education. She was initially tutored at home, as there were no schools for girls in Shiraz at the time. By the time she was married off at the young age of fifteen, schooling for girls had been introduced, and she insisted on going to school and finishing at least her formal elementary education. As a boy of five, Golestan accompanied his mother to her all-girls school. When I asked him about her last name, he said it was Golestan. I thought he had misunderstood my question. I meant her maiden name, I told him. His response was yet another poignant metaphor for

---

16. I have discussed Kaveh, his childhood, and Golestan's relationship with him in an extended interview. See Abbas Milani, "Ravayat Golestan az Kaveh" [Golestan's narrative of Kaveh], *Nilufar Abi*, special issue on Kaveh, Bahman (Esfand 1395/ February–March 2018), pp. 22–24

the changes Golestan has witnessed in his life. He said that when his mother was born, nobody in Iran had last names or birth certificates. By the time they both became mandatory, she was already married and so took her husband's last name and became Fatemeh Golestan. He has also told me about how, when he was a child, his playmates in the neighborhood would converge on his house, around sunset, to watch in amazement as he flipped an electric switch and the room lit up! His childhood home was one of the first in the city to have electricity. Now in Iran, there is electricity in virtually every village, and there are over a hundred million smartphones in a population of eighty-five million people. To his credit, Golestan has not just witnessed and chronicled in his films and writings some of these extraordinary transformations, but has diligently attempted to keep abreast of them.

On his father's side, Golestan came from a long line of clerics. His paternal grandfather was an esteemed and defiant nonconformist ayatollah—exiled by Reza Shah—while his father began as a cleric before going on to become a prominent secular journalist. For many years, he published a liberal newspaper called *Golestan*. He was an early champion of education for women—an issue hotly rejected by most of the clergy in the country. Golestan's father was at once a dedicated intellectual and a dapper Epicurean, with a gargantuan appetite for the pleasures of life.

Young Golestan's home was a veritable literary and political salon, affording Ebrahim the chance to meet many of

Ebrahim Golestan's parents and his two brothers and sisters.

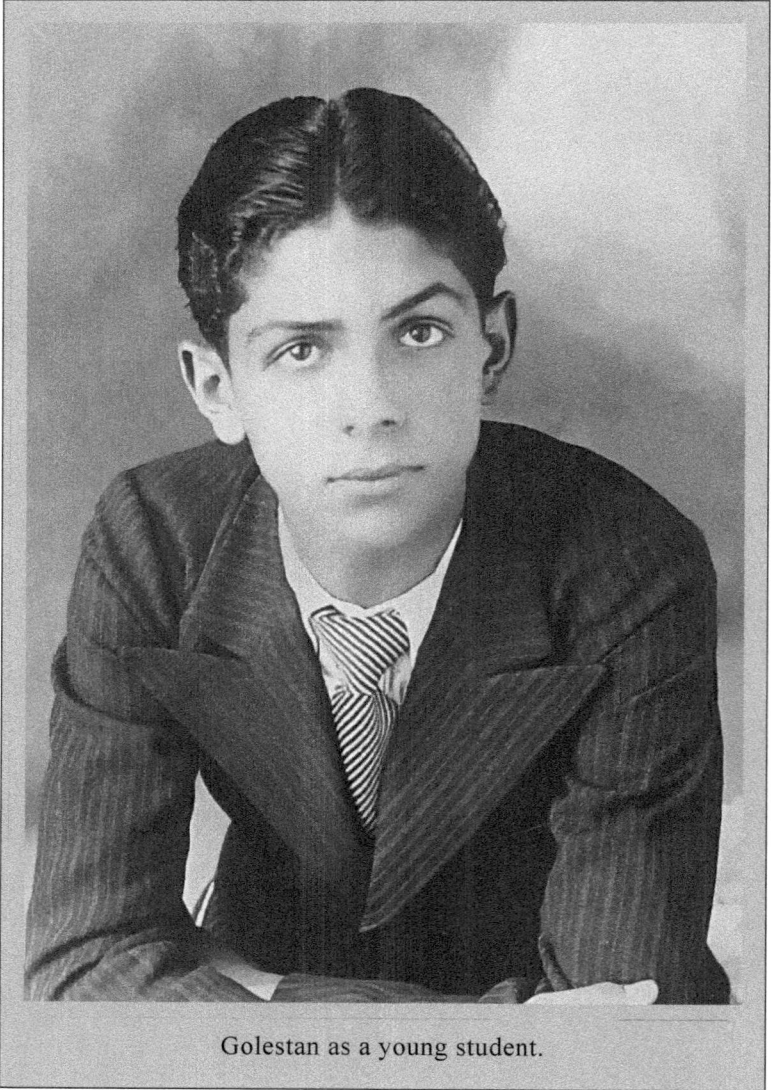

Golestan as a young student.

the celebrated writers and poets of the time. He also began to satisfy his insatiable curiosity about the world by devouring his father's books. At the behest of his father, who was learning French, Ebrahim too learnt French, becoming fluent before he

Ebrahim Golestan with his father and wife Fakhri.

left high school. At the same time, he was an avid athlete, holding a national record in track events for many years. Golestan's first published essays—including one in praise of the short stories of Mohammad Hejazi (1900–1974)[17] that caught the attention of the famed author and brought about the first meeting between the two[18]—appeared in his father's newspaper.

Golestan was educated first in Shiraz and then, in 1939, was sent to Tehran where he lived with this uncle and fell in love with his cousin—Fakhri. Eventually, they married and Golestan left the Faculty of Law and Political Science at Tehran

17. An Iranian novelist, short-story writer, playwright, essayist, translator, and member of the senate.
18. Golestan was in high school at the time. He was standing in the hall as a punishment for some "impertinent" question when the principal found him and told him that Mr. Hejazi wanted to meet him. In later years the two met many more times, under very different circumstances. It is interesting to note that while most "progressive" critics have dismissed Hejazi for what they call his "romantic" or even frivolous stories, Golestan has always praised the quality of his works.

University where he had begun to study. His defiant curiosity, literary disposition, and gradual leaning towards the radical new ideas that were spreading in an Iran still occupied by the Allied forces, were stifled within the stolid confines of a very traditional law faculty.

As with everything else in his life, before he jumped into the political maelstrom by joining the Tudeh Party—the *de facto* communist party of Iran created under the tutelage of the "Big Brother" of the USSR—he began by reading books on the subject, this time by Marx and Lenin. He translated into Persian and self-published two important essays from the Marxist–Leninist pantheon. One was his lucid translation of the essay Stalin had written on dialectical materialism in *History of the Communist Party of the Soviet Union (Bolsheviks)*, considered at the time to be the bible of Marxism–Leninism.[19] The other work Golestan translated was Lenin's essay on Marxism.[20] By the time he joined the party, he had already published these essays. One of the most detailed descriptions of his life in the party can be found in *Mokhtar and His Time*. An engrossing account, it also sheds light on the indispensable role his wife, Fakhri, herself a dedicated party member, had in this activism.

It is part of the paradox of Golestan that, while he translated these texts, he joined a party whose ideology was quintessentially

---

19. For a discussion of the book as "history" and "philosophy," see Leszaek Kolakowski, *Main Currents of Marxism*, trans. P.S. Falla, 3 vols (New York: Norton, 2005), pp. 822–67 (translated into Persian by Abbas Milani). For a detailed account of the personal role Stalin played in drafting and publishing the book (in millions of copies), see Stephen Kotkin, *Stalin: Waiting for Hitler, 1929–1941* (New York: Penguin, 2017), pp. 569–72. For a Persian translation of the section by Stalin on dialectical materialism, see Joseph Stalin, *Dialectic*. [Dialectical Materialism] trans. Ebrahim Golestan (Tehran: no pub., 1323/1943).

20. Lenin, *Osul Marxism* [Principles of Marxism], trans. Ebrahim Golestan (Tehran: no pub., 1323/1943).

Fakhri Golestan

Stalinist and whose dogma on literary criticism came from the infamous Russian hack Andrei Zhdanov, who saw literature as a mere tool of party propaganda. Golestan used his role as an editor of *Rahbar*, the party newspaper to publish essays on writers like Ernest Hemingway—hardly a Zhdanovian favorite. Golestan is rightly proud of the changes he brought to not only the content of the paper, but to the size of its readership, making it at the time one of the most widely read newspapers in the country.

A telling anecdote about the dominant literary culture of the party and its incongruence with Golestan's sensibilities was described to me by Golestan himself. The year was 1946, and it was Nowruz, the Persian new year, when family and friends visit each other and exchange gifts. Golestan had gone to visit

Maryam Firuz—the quintessential "red aristocrat" and a scion of the Farmanfarma family, who had joined the party soon after its creation in 1941 and stayed loyal to the end of her life. Maryam gave Golestan a copy of a new Modern Library edition of Dostoyevsky's *Brothers Karamazov*. When Ehsan Tabari—the storied party theorist and the chief peddler of Zhdanov literary theories in Persian—saw the book, he chastised Maryam for presenting such a "decadent" work as a gift. The reactionary audacity of such a *fatwa* is matched only by the paradoxical optimism of an artist like Golestan, who not only joins that party but uses its magazines and newspapers to offer his starkly different view of literature.

Another paradoxical aspect of Golestan's life in the party is first the fervor of his activism as a member, and then his early recognition that the party was too dependent on dogma and the Soviet Union to be a vessel of liberation in Iran. He was thus one of the first prominent members of the party to part company with it. His close friend and noted economist Eprime Eshag (1918–98) was amongst the first members to split from the party and write a critique of its structure and policies.[21] While Golestan ultimately distanced himself from the party, he did not join the ranks of those who wrote about the "God that failed" and took on Marxism as the "new opium" of the masses.[22]

---

21. He wrote two seminal critiques of the party before leaving Iran for England, where he eventually became an economist at Oxford University. The first, echoing Lenin's famous essay, was called "What is to be Done?", and the second was entitled "The Tudeh Party at a Crossroads."

22. In 1949, a number of prominent intellectuals who had joined the communist movement and had grown disgruntled with it published a book famously entitled *The God that Failed*. See *The God that Failed*, ed. Richard Crossman (New York: Columbia University Press, 2001). In 1955, Raymond Aron, the influential French sociologist, published a book that parodied Marx's famous phrase about religion being the opium of the masses, referring to Marxism

By the time Golestan joined the Tudeh Party, he was affluent. He had earlier become a purchasing agent for the American forces in Tehran and through hard work and diligence had earned some 300,000 tomans—a hefty sum at the time. Once he joined the party, and with the avid support of Fakhri, he donated virtually the entire sum to the party coffers. He has no regrets about the time, energy, and financial support he gave to promote the cause of the party. In fact, more than once in his nineties, he has confided that during those brief years of activism he had, more than ever, the comforting feeling of being productively and passionately engaged in a worthy cause. Nevertheless, the allure of literature, photography, and freedom of thought, together with family obligations and his own sense of patriotism, combined to trump the joys of that kind of "engaged" activism. He left the party in 1947 but his attachment to Marxism, to elements of party ideology, his criticism of party leaders like Tabari and his support of others, particularly the controversial former general secretary, Noureddin Kianouri, has endured into his centennial year.

From his early youth, Golestan was keenly interested in photography; and when he decided to leave the Tudeh Party, he became a professional photographer. By then, he had already published his first collection of short stories. After 1954, when a consortium of Western oil companies took over the operation of the Iranian oil industry, Golestan joined the new company and was put in charge of making educational films about the oil industry.[23] In 1959, after severing ties with the oil consortium, he set up his own studio and negotiated the buy-out of the equipment

---

as the opium of the intellectuals. See Raymond Aron, *The Opium of the Intellectuals*, trans. Harvey Mansfield et al. (New Brunswick: Transaction Publishers, 2001).

23. A detailed filmography of all of Golestan's films has been provided in Farid Esmailpour, *La genèse du cinéma d'auteur iranien: Ebrahim Golestan* (Paris: Éditions L'Harmattan, 2017), pp. 143–4.

he had purchased to make the documentaries. Augmenting this equipment with much new equipment he purchased, his studio became the most sophisticated center for film making in Iran. At the same time, well into the late 1950s, he enjoyed a near-monopoly in the lucrative market of supplying film clips and photos to the increasingly large Western media, and to assuaging the endless appetite of Western television for images of Iran.

A number of other prominent poets and actors worked at the studio, including Forough Farrokhzad (1934–67), by then a famous poet with a reputation for fierce assertive independence. In 1957, Forough and Golestan began an intense love affair that continued until the end of her tragically short life. Farrokhzad's most mature and productive poetry coincided with the years of her relationship with Golestan—regarded as the most celebrated and discussed love affair in modern Persian literature. In her pioneering literary biography of Forough, Farzaneh Milani, with access to some of Forough's letters to Golestan, reveals the depth of the poet's love for Golestan.[24] Milani has even suggested that, owing to his pervasive presence in the poetry of Forough Farokhzad, Golestan is easily the most cherished beloved man in modern Persian poetry.[25] It is a measure of Fakhri Golestan's magnanimity and, by all indication, her enduring love for her husband, that their marriage continued in spite of the gossip that the tempestuous affair generated, and the pressures it must have created in her life. It was during this period that Golestan produced Farrokhzad's masterpiece documentary *The House is Black (1962)*. Forough's death in 1967 added a new, unbearable burden to the sense of exile and estrangement Golestan had already felt in Iran. After her death, friends talked of his

---

24. Farzaneh Milani, *Forough Farrhzad: zendegi nameh-ye adabi* [Forough Farokhzad: A Literary Biography] (Toronto: Persian Circle, 2016).

25. Farzaneh Milani, interview with author, January 7, 2004.

Forugh Farrokhzad photo taken by Ebrahim Golestan

debilitating grief;[26] shortly thereafter, he left Iran, beginning his physical exile.

---

26. Abolghassem Sa'idi, interview with author, Paris, August 2, 2002. I learnt about Golestan's grief from several sources, including Golestan, in his *Letter to Simin*, Sa'idi, the prominent painter and Sadeq Chubaq who, canceled a long planned trip at the last minute, fearing that his friend Golestan might kill himself.

The gradual tightening of political screws in Iran was another reason Golestan chose to leave the country. It was also an educational journey. All his life, he had been, essentially, an autodidact. He left Iran and spent the first "six months just visiting museums and going to theaters and concerts."[27] The only time he returned to Iran for any length of time was to make *Mysteries of the Ghost Valley (1974)*. Not long after finishing the film, he sold his studio, leaving his wife and children behind (along with much of the money from the sale), and made his permanent home in England. By then, with his prize-winning documentaries and his feature films,[28] he had helped make Iranian cinema the object of sustained curiosity by film critics and film festivals, throughout the world. His documentaries, whether describing the crown jewels or the oil industry, combine stunning imagery with terse and beautiful prose, an attention to language that has its roots, partially at least, in his sensibilities as a writer of fiction. Even in his fiction he was an iconoclast in both form and substance.

In the sixties and seventies, advocates of "committed art" and "socialist realism" favored fiction that was simple and bereft of formal complexity. Golestan instead wrote stories that were as structurally intricate as the worlds they depicted. He believed that there was just one right way to articulate an idea or an image, and that it was the responsibility of the artist to "work hard and honestly to arrive at this single form; other forms are characterless, and inadequate."[29] Through experience, he had come to recognize that "there is no difference between the shallow views of the Left or the Right";[30] one makes literature the tool of the party and history, the other wants it to be subservient to God, king, country, or leader. Neither in his art nor in his life

---

27. Ebrahim Golestan, interview with author, August 9, 2003.
28. For a detailed account of Golestan's documentaries and the prizes he has won, see Esmaeelpour, *La genèse du cinema d'auteur iranien.*
29. Golestan, *Gofteha*, p. 154.
30. Ibid., p. 131.

did Golestan follow the dictates of this Manichaean vision. Advocates of this vision had nothing but disdain for anyone who worked in the Shah's regime. In his appraisal of those who worked for the regime, Golestan took a more personal and pragmatic approach, happy to work with those he liked and found to be contributing to a better tomorrow, and criticizing those he disliked and deemed destructive. In his view, some working in the Shah's government showed considerable intellectual power and respect for human dignity. Though "caught in the strait-jacket of their time," they were nonetheless "committed to the comfort and dignity of the people in their community." In the long run, they were far more effective in serving their country than "the impotent phrasemongers who, in their desperation, incurable jealousy and malicious envy,"[31] did nothing other than engage in futile and detrimental nihilism.

This pragmatic approach did not mean that Golestan has pulled any punches in criticizing those aspects of the reality he found wanting. His film *Mysteries of the Ghost Valley*[32] is often seen as the most daring critique of the status quo in Iran in the years before the revolution. But his other works are no less blunt in their censure. His film on Iran's crown jewels (1966), commissioned by the Iranian Central Bank, is a good example of his approach. In the voice-over commentary for the film, he describes these jewels as souvenirs of closed minds, "besotted by toys. Souvenirs of men bedazzled with glitz and glamour ... Only three writing pens in the midst of hundreds of thousands of precious artifacts." He describes the Qajar dynasty's indifference to global and domestic developments: "A history of three hundred years of indifference, written in the glamorous syntax of

---

31. Ibid., p. 30.
32. For a political reading of the film, and an attempt to decode its many allusions to contemporary figures and events, see Milani, *The Persian Sphinx*, pp. 243–63.

jewels."[33] And he ends by praising Reza Shah—uncommon for "progressive" intellectuals of the time—for using these jewels as reserve assets for the national currency.

The pith and parsimony of Golestan's descriptions may themselves be construed as one of his enduring contributions to Persian literature. His prose has often been praised for its beauty precision and poetry. It is also deeply democratic in nature. He not only uses the language of various strata of society to create polyphony in his narratives, but he also demands the active participation of the reader in giving meaning to the text. He incorporates the poetry and music of conversation, its crescendos, its omissions, and its silences. Just as the correct reading of a poem requires cognizance and command of its rhyme and meter, so the correct reading of Golestan's prose requires familiarity with its special rhythms. In describing what he calls "clean prose," he emphasizes that, in writing such prose, the most important thing is "to take as our model the pattern of an oral conversation, that has the effervescence of a living organism, and the liveliness of effervescence."[34] Indeed, it is the complex, calculated, and choreographed stylistic nuances of his prose, the significance of not just syntax but the syncopation of each sentence, that makes translating his work a daunting task.

Golestan's "Encounter with Dylan Thomas" (pp. 31–113) features all these tropes, along with the dynamic flow and tempo of a play, particularly in its dialogue. Part of the conversation with Thomas is about the difficulties of translation. For me, the illuminating experience of translating Golestan's text confirms his theory, but even more importantly, it reaffirms the sheer joy of reading and appreciating a narrative as tight in its structure and as striking in its imagery as any Persian rug.

---

33. Golestan, *Gofteha*, p. 177.
34. Ibid., p. 224.

There is another aspect of Golestan's language and images that renders them particularly modern. Following in the footsteps of such early masters as Gorgani and Nezami, Golestan infuses some of his stories and films with startlingly frank and surprisingly beautiful depictions of erotic desire.[35] Contrary to the claim of commentators who suggest that writing about carnal desire, and genres such as the novel and the short story, are specifically Western, Golestan is among the handful of Iranian writers and thinkers who have refused to accept this Eurocentric assumption. In his first feature film, *Brick and Mirror (1965)*, for example, he dared show a tastefully choreographed erotic encounter between a man and woman who were not married. In this encounter, the woman is the assertive partner, and Golestan pointedly uses as a backdrop a poster of a similar scene from Iran's mytho-history depicting a man and woman in an intimate moment. But film critics and cultural commissars lambasted Golestan for this daring scene, the poet Ahmad Shamloo going so far as to calling the film "pornographic."[36]

Golestan is aware of the intricate and intimate relationship between language and thought, and how easily both may become degraded, as he believes they did in mid-twentieth-century Iran. He knows that "when the mind is not living ... the stimuli and tools of the mind also fall into disuse, as they have in our case. Our language was impoverished by our mindlessness,

---

35. For an erudite and eye-opening account of the history of erotica in Persian letters—particularly those of the period I have referred to as the age of Iran's aborted modernity—see Jalal Khaleghi Motlagh, "Tan kameh sarai dar adab-e farsi" [Erotica in Persian Letters], *Iran Shenasi* 1 (Spring 1375/1996), pp. 15–55.

36. Upon the publication of *Encounters in the Season of Encounter*, I wrote a brief review of the often acrimonious attitude of many critics towards Golestan's books and films. See Abbas Milani, "Barkhord ba barkhordha-ye Golestan" [Encounter with Golestan's Encounters], *BBC Persian*, https://www.bbc.com/Persian/blog-viewpoints-60444658.

and this poverty itself led to further mindlessness."[37] Similar ideas are evident also in his discussion with Thomas. Only by transcending the reification[38] of our mind and language—this tendency to attribute to creations of our own minds supernatural powers—can we begin to experience genuine modernity. Many of Golestan's stories and films are explorations of the ebb and flow of this transcendence. Some of the most fervently argued parts of the "An Encounter with Dylan Thomas" is also about the same issue. (pp. 85–96)

One of the main obstacles on the way to this "transcendence" in Iran according to Golestan, is the pervasive belief in a messiah. Disenfranchised people are invariably prone to a deep yearning for a savior who will come and lead them to a promised land. In several stories, Golestan tackles this issue, offering gripping, albeit sad, tales about the pervasive hold this kind of false hope has on many Iranians. In one story he writes: "waiting means not living in the moment."[39] He describes the lingering habit of some Iranians in small towns who, in anticipation of the expected Mahdi, saddle a horse "every day, early in the morning ... in case the messiah arrives."[40] In another story, one of the characters laments this long futile wait for the messiah, and defiantly declares: "when the messiah forgets to arrive" on time, delaying his arrival until a moment in history when "the horse is no longer a means of travel," he, too, in return, reserves the right

---

37. Golestan, *Gofteha*, pp. 112–13.
38. For a discussion of "reification," see Georg Lukács, *History and Class Consciousness*, trans. Rodney Livingstone (London: Merlin Press, 1971), pp. 83–110. Golestan's discussion with Thomas is, in its genealogy, from that same Marxist tradition. Golestan had not read any of Lukács at the time of that encounter. In fact, little of Lukács was even available in English then.
39. Ebrahim Golestan, *Mad va meh* [The Tide and the Fog] (New Jersey, Rowzan, 1994), p. 173.
40. Ibid., p. 173.

"to doubt [the messiah's] saving powers."[41] Though the stories were written several decades ago, their discussion of messianism could easily be regarded as a piercing critique of the messianism that endures in some elements of Iranian society today.

Religion has been the chief, though not the sole, source of this messianism, and Golestan offers a bold critique of its role in his short story "Being or Being an Icon: A Puppet Show in Two Acts." In the story, two brothers, Hassan and Hossein, are waiting in the desert with their father. After a while, their mother arrives, riding with a man astride a camel. Soon we learn that the stranger is not a "dirty dog of an Armenian,"[42] but a Frenchman. The "dirty dog" is an obvious ironic reference to the common belief among some Muslims in Iran that dogs are incorrigibly "unclean" (*najes*). Armenians, as non-Muslims, are also considered by some believers as *najes*. This Frenchman, however, turns out to be the inventor of the camera—one of the most potent metaphors of modernity. Gradually the intended identity of the other characters becomes clear.

Hossein, constantly complaining of thirst, unmistakably reminds us of Imam Hossein, one of the most venerable figures in Shiism and the ultimate martyr of a religion that defines itself, at least partially, by the power of its martyrs. The story of his battle (in 680 CE) with the army of the Caliph is the most powerful source of Shiism's passion plays. Hossein had come to Karbala to claim the mantle of the prophet, and his army of seventy-two followers was decimated by the superior force of Yazid, the ruling caliph. But in the world of Golestan's story, Hossein, rather than being praised by Hassan for his heroism, is called a "masochist" by his more rational brother, who takes a dim view of such recklessness: "sometimes you make an ass of yourself, and sometimes you make an ass of others. You have

---

41. Ibid., p. 174.
42. Ebrahim Golestan, *Jooy va divar va teshneh* [The Stream and the Wall and the Thirsty], (New Jersey, Rozan, 1994), p. 144.

Ebrahim Golestan with his longtime companion Ashi Esfandiari.

passion, but you don't have brains. It's like you were born only to become a martyr … You are more of a martyr than a human being."[43] Reflecting Golestan's own self-assertive intellect, Hassan's advice to his brother is to forgo the temptations of martyrdom, and instead "depend on your own brain; your own intelligence; even if it goes against what other people think."[44]

Golestan is a man with a contagious appetite for life and all it offers, while remaining outwardly stoic in response to its tragedies. At his centennial, he remains an omnivore in his taste in books. A scholarly biography of Stalin by Stephen Katkin, a new book on Shakespeare by Harold Bloom, or the most recent collection of short stories by a hitherto unknown Iranian writer are all equally fascinating to him. In music, he is a true aficionado. A Furtwangler performance of a Beethoven symphony puts him in a trance-like state, with eyes closed, occasionally wet around the edges with tears, his hands moving gently as if he were conducting. The scene captures the very majesty and magic of music. More than once I have been tempted to take a picture of him in such a moment, but I have refrained every time, lest I disrupt the epiphany evident in his face. His knowledge of the history of painting in Iran and the West is legendary. He has a knack of picking Iranian masters and masterpieces before they become the darling of galleries, making him one of the most successful collectors of modern Iranian art. A good bottle of wine—of which he is an experienced connoisseur—a walk in the green, rainy English countryside, where he lives in an impeccably restored nineteenth-century mansion, or a moment

---

43. Ibid., p. 151.
44. Ibid., p. 158.

of quiet contemplation on the balcony of a small two-bedroom apartment in Nice, bring out in him an ebullient *joie de vivre* that is only subtly tempered by the melancholy that comes with wisdom, and with suffering the "slings and arrows of outrageous fortune." He is the embodiment of an eminent artist who has made an enduring and increasing impact on modern Iranian culture. His centennial is a moment of celebration for all who cherish this culture and hope that it may see happier days.

Photo courtesy of Yasmin Zahedi.

EBRAHIM GOLESTAN

An Encounter with Dylan Thomas

برخوردها
در
زمانهٔ برخورد

Translated by
Abbas Milani

تقویم می‌گفت در زمستانیم اما گرما و حالت هوا بهاری بود. در چشم‌انداز چیزی نبود جز خط سبزِ تارِ گردآلود از نخل‌های حاشیهٔ شط دور با دشت صاف که در خاك آن نمك راهی به ریشه و روییدنی نداده بود و خاك، پف کرده از نم و نم بعد پیش آفتاب خشکیده، پوك بود و قشر نازكش از کم‌ترین فشارِ قدم می‌شکست، پا در آن فرو می‌رفت. محله‌یی که من در آن اتاق داشتم میان آن بیابان بود، محلهٔ اتاق‌های خالی بسیار، دورازشهر. من خواسته بودم در آن اتاق داشته باشم‌چون درست دور بود از شهر، دور از بو و دود و از صدا و رفت‌وآمدها، از بندر و اداره‌ها و پالایشگاه و ساکنان معدودش، کارمندان مجرد شرکت، در اول هر صبح می‌رفتند سر کار روزانه یا برمی‌گشتند از کارهای شب‌نوبت برای خوابیدن. آنجا، تمام روز، دنیای خالیِ ساکت بود. اتاقم فقط برای خواندن و نوشتن بود، جایی که خانه بود جای دیگر بود.

کار اداری من از غروب بود تا نیمه‌شب، ولی از صبح می‌آمدم تا ظهر در این جای دنج کار می‌کردم برای خودم ـــ کتاب می‌خواندم، یا می‌نوشتم یا نوشته‌هایم را خط می‌زدم می‌انداختم دور. برای کردن این کار دومی به کار اولی نیاز بود اما غرض از کار اولی دومی نبود، البته، هرچند حاجت به آن همیشه بود، هست. آنجا کسی سراغ من نمی‌آمد جز رانندهٔ اداره که هر روز ظهرها می‌آمد مرا می‌برد و هر روز صبح‌ها می‌آوردم. حالا، یکی ـ دوساعتی از آوردنم گذشته و یك‌ساعتی

The calendar said it was winter, yet the heat and mood of the weather were more springlike. On the horizon, there was nothing save an opaque dusty green line of palms on the banks of the far-away river, with a flat plain in whose terrain salt had given no quarter to roots or vegetation of any kind. And each morning the earth became swollen with dew, which, warmed by the rising sun, created a thin outer shell that would shatter at the lightest footstep, plunging your foot deep into the soil beneath. The neighborhood in which I had a room in stood in the middle of that plane. A neighborhood of many empty rooms. Far away from the city. I had asked to have a room there because it was away from the city, away from its smells and smoke, and from its sounds and its hustle and bustle. Away from the port and the offices and the oil refinery and its few employees. Company employees who were single left for their daily work early each morning or returned from their night shifts to sleep. There, all day, it was an empty and quiet world. My room there was only for reading and writing. The place I called home, happened to be elsewhere.

My office work was from afternoon to midnight. But I came to my room in this cozy place in the morning and worked until noon for myself. I read books; I wrote or crossed out what I had written and threw it away. To do the latter, the former was needed, though the intent of the former was not the latter, yet the need was always there, and always would be. Nobody sought me there except the driver who came every day at noon to pick me up and, every morning, dropped me off there. And now, a couple

به بردنم مانده، در می‌زدند. هیچ‌کس هم نبود از آشناهایم که بداند من آن‌جایم، یا جای خصوصی‌ام آن‌جاست، جز همین دو رانندهٔ اداره. سرک کشیدم از میان شیشه‌های پنجره دیدم یکی از همان دو راننده است. در را که باز کردم گفت رئیس گفته است بیایم. پرسیدم در این وقتِ بی‌وقتی چه‌کار به من دارد. گفت از لندن مهمانی آمده است در اداره که می‌خواهند من ببینمش.

رفتم.

وقتی که رسیدیم رئیس رفته بود. رفتم در اتاق معاون ایرانی‌اش که اسمش محمد صالح ابوسعیدی بود و، در آن‌وقت، از پشت میز مقام معاونت مشغول شرکت بود در سکوت کامل حضار. حضار که جز یك نفر همه از کارمندان اداره‌مان بودند از رسیدنم تبسم مؤدبانهٔ مرسوم را نشان دادند، تمام جز همان یك نفر که ناشناس بود و کماییش چاق و گرد بود و نوكِ بینیِ بسیار گردِ گُندهِ داشت که من فکر کردم لابد همان مهمانِ ازانگلستان‌رسیده است. او با وجود برق هوشمندی در نگاه‌های فرزِ جوینده‌اش انگار ناتوان مانده بود از جواب‌به‌خودداد‌ن که این‌ها کی‌اند و او کجاست و جایی که هست چرا جور دیگری است از آن‌چه او می‌شناسد و دیده است؛ انگار پشت لفاف غربت خود گیر کرده بود که کنجکاوی‌هایش داشت جا وامی‌گذاشت به خمیازهٔ دهان‌بسته.

از همکاران اداریم آن‌جا دکتر حمید نطقی بود و منوچهر مستشاری و عبدالله وزیری و ابوالقاسم حالت. یك آقای مهتدی هم بود اما این را که او آیا آن روز حتماً‌آن‌جا بود یا نبود درست به یاد ندارم. هم‌چنان که اسم کوچك او را، هرچند هرگز از یادم نرفته است آن گفته که یك روز از زبان او دررفت. آن یك روز ظهر بود و تابستان، و ما، چهار ـ پنج‌تائی چپیده در اتومبیل اداره برای نهار می‌رفتیم و سر راه، وقتی که ایستادیم تا یکی‌مان پیاده شود، دیدیم چند گنجشك بر شاخه‌های نازكِ آونگ‌واِر دربادجنبنده دراز خاردارِ استوائی میموزا جیك‌جیك می‌کردند و می‌جَستند. آقای مهتدی

of hours after I had been dropped off and an hour before I was due to be picked up, there came a knock at the door. None of my acquaintances knew I was there, or that this was my hideaway, except, of course, the two drivers from the office. I peeked out of a window and saw that it was indeed one of the drivers. As I opened the door, he said the boss had told him to come. I asked what the boss wanted with me at that unseemly hour. He said a guest had arrived from London at the office, and they wanted me to meet him.

I went.

When I arrived, the boss had already left. I went to the office of his Iranian deputy, whose name was Mohammad Saleh Abusaidi, and at that moment, from behind the deputy's desk, he was, along with the rest of those present, completely silent. Those present were all, except one, colleagues from our office, and upon my arrival, they offered the customary polite grin; all, of course, except the stranger among them who was more or less obese and rotund, and had a big lump of a nose and I assumed must be the guest who had just arrived from England. He, in spite of a spark of cleverness in his quick and searching eyes, had apparently failed to answer his own questions about who these people were, and where he was, and why this place was so different from any he knew and had seen, and thus he appeared stuck behind a mask of acting like a stranger and his curiosity had given way to a series of barely suppressed yawns.

Of my colleagues, Dr. Hamid Notghi, Manouchehr Mostashari, Abdullah Vaziri, and Abolgassem Halat were there. Mr. Mohtadi was also a colleague, but I don't quite recall whether or not he was there that day. I also don't recall his first name, though I have never forgotten the words that one day slipped from his tongue. It was a summer day, at noon, and four or five of us had squeezed into an office car and were going for lunch. When we stopped for one of us to get out, we saw a few sparrows sitting on a thin, windswept, long thorny branch of a tropical mimosa

به آنها گفت «گنجشك‌ها، ما این‌جا اسیر پوینت و امتیاز و امید اضافه‌حقوق‌مان هستیم، شما که نیستید چرا پَر نمی‌زنید از این هوای گرم پُر از بوی بد بیرون؟» آقای مهتدی رفیق سالیان دراز و صمیمی آقای ابوسعیدی بود جوری که در موارد اساسیِ گوناگون همراه و مثل هم بودند ازجمله در امر سعی مستمرشان به کسب بسط دانش و فرهنگ‌شان از منبع ماهانه‌شان، ریدرز دایجست. منوچهر مستشاری تنیس‌باز ماهر بود که عشقش به این بازی زیادتر بود از مهارتش در این بازی. دکتر نطقی که از دانشگاه استانبول رتبهٔ دکتری در حقوق سیاسی گرفته بود تمام نطق‌های آتاتورك را از حفظ داشت و تمام ترجمه‌های پیتی گریلی ایتالیائی را خوانده بود به ترکی، و جز کتاب‌خواندن و بعد از ساعت‌های اداره توی‌خانه‌ماندن و همراه با زن بسیار مهربان ساده و آرامش باز کتاب‌خواندن تفریحی یا ورزشی نداشت، و بسیار محتاط و تندفهم و تیزبین بود و مسلط به آن‌چه طلب می‌کرد اما هرگز نمی‌دیدی چیزی طلب کند که ندارد، حتی اگر می‌خواستی دید، حتی اگر طلب می‌کرد. حالت هم، ابوالقاسم، که سر راه بازگشتنش از بمبئی، که رفته بود آن‌جا همراه بانو دلکش برای صفحه‌پرکردن و گفتارهای تصنیف‌های خالدی را به‌نظم‌درآوردن، وقتی کشتی‌شان می‌رسد به خرمشهر، می‌رود به دیدار مصطفی فاتح که سرشناس و مدیر مؤثر ایرانی در دستگاه شرکت بود تا کاری از او در ادارهٔ انتشارات نفت می‌گیرد. کارش در دستگاه نفت نظم‌نوشتن بود از ضرب‌المثل‌های فارسی و انگلیسی و عربی تا کلمات قصار بزرگان

tree, chirping and jumping with the pendulum-like movement of the branch. Addressing the sparrows, Mr. Mohtadi said, "We here are slaves to points and promotions and hopes of a salary increase. You are not. Why don't you just fly away from these hot, foul smelly climes?" Mr. Mohtadi was for many years such a close friend of Mr. Abusaidi that, in many essential respects, they were indistinguishable, including in their persistent effort to gain and increase their knowledge from their monthly source, the *Reader's Digest.* Manouchehr Mostashari was a capable tennis player whose love of the game exceeded his excellence in it. Dr. Notghi had received a doctorate in political science from Istanbul University. He knew by heart all of Atatürk's speeches and had read, in Turkish, all the works of the Italian Peti Greely, and aside from reading books, and staying home after the work day with his very kind and simple and quiet wife, and again reading books, he engaged in no other activity or recreation, and he was very conservative, and quick-witted and perceptive and competent in every venture, but you never saw him seek what he didn't have, even if you were to observe him, or indeed even if he was so inclined. Abolgassem Halat, too, had accompanied Dame Delkash[1] to Bombay to record some music and versifying some of the narratives in Khaledi's songs,[2] and upon their return, when their ship reached Khoramshahr, Halat visited Mostafah Fateh, who was a well-known and effective Iranian manager in the oil company, and asked him for a job in the company's publishing office. In that capacity, his work was wide-ranging, from versifying the aphorisms of great men and common expressions in Persian and English and Arabic, to

---

1. One of Iran's most iconic woman vocalists, and occasional actor. Born in 1925 she had a unique voice, at once velvety but assertive. She died in 2004 in relative poverty.
2. Mehdi Khaledi was a master violinist and composer who worked with many of the masters of classical music.

و برگزیده‌های نهج‌البلاغه و شوخی‌های رایج روزانه که در آن روزها هنوز به‌شان «جُك» نمی‌گفتند، «جُك» که همان «جوك» انگلیسی است، و این‌ها تمام دست‌مایه‌های حرفهٔ او بودند، و حرفه‌اش همین روزانه نظم‌نوشتن بود و با روزانه نظم‌نوشتن صیقل به حرفه‌اش می‌داد. حالت همیشه با رفاه روح و درویشی در کناره‌ها می‌ماند، از کناره‌ها می‌رفت و خوش می‌نشست وقتی که می‌نشست و خوش با خودش، ساده، با حضور ذهن و ذهن محتاطش زندگی می‌کرد. با کم‌توقعی خود را آزاد نگه می‌داشت بی آن‌که آزادبودن از حدود شخصی او رد شود، یا بخواهدش که شعاری برای دیگران باشد. با شیر خشك ماست می‌انداخت برای نهار روزانه‌اش. شب‌ها، هرشب، یا می‌رفت به باشگاه ایران یا به مهمانی، در هر دو حال به مهمانی، به بذله‌گوئی برای دوستان و آشنایانش. سلیم و بی‌آزار بود و از این بابت مانندش را میان کسانی که می‌شناختم نمی‌شناختم، اما ازبس که از من و پزشک‌نیا و دکتر نطقی طرفداری شنیده بود از نیما افتاده بود به این فکر که نظم بسازد به صورت نوشته‌یی شعر نیمائی، کاری که دیگران هم بعدها کردند، بعضی کمی از او بهتر بعضی زیادتر از او بدتر، بی آن‌که فرق شعر از نظم را ملتفت باشند بدانند شعر در شکل نوشته نیست، با شکل نوشته نیست که شعر می‌گردد. اکنون رسیده

offering selections of *Nahj al-Balagheh*[3] or everyday gags—or what in today's English are called jokes, though in those days nobody called them that. And these were all the stuff of his profession, and his job there consisted of these versifications, and with these daily versifications he polished his profession. Easygoing and contented and with monkish habits, Halat always remained on the margins, and moved on the margins. Comfortable in his own skin, he was great company every time he chose to be with you, and he lived simply, at one with his own agile mind and his conservative bent. With low expectations, he maintained his independence without allowing this independence stray beyond his own private domain or to become a slogan for others. He used powdered milk to make yogurt for his lunch each day. In the evenings, every night, he went either to the Iran Club or to a party, in both cases as a guest, where he regaled his friends and acquaintances with jokes. He was hearty and harmless in this respect and among those I knew, I knew no one like him. Having so often heard me and Pezeshknia[4] and Dr. Notghi praise the poetry of Nima,[5] he decided to compose a piece in rhymed prose instead of verse imitating a Nima poem, something that others tried later, some a bit better than him, others a lot worse, all without knowing the difference between poetry and verse, and without knowing that what makes a poem is not the form of the

---

3. *Nahj al-Balagha* (The Path of Eloquence) is the best-known collection of sermons, letters, and sayings attributed to Ali ibn Abi Talib, first Shia Imam, the cousin and son-in-law of the prophet, Muhammad.

4. Houshang Pezeshknia was a modernist painter and a friend and colleague of Golestan. In his writings, Golestan has praised the modernist innovations of Pezeshknia and lamgented the fact that his infatuation with becoming a "progressive" painter hampered his growth. Pezeshknia died young, in 1979. He was born in 1918 or 1919.

5. Nima (1897–1960), is by near consensus the first and one of the most influential modernist poets of Iran.

بودم میان این آشناهای اتفاقی که آقای ابوسعیدی مرا به آن مرد انگلیسی به‌انگلیسی و او را به من به‌فارسی شناسانید گفت «این آقای توماس است که گویا در انگلستان شعر می‌گوید و حالا آمده است برای نوشتنِ یک فیلمِ مطالعاتی به عمل بیاورد.»

از همین «مطالعات به‌عمل‌آوردن»ش پیداست که این‌ها را به‌فارسی گفت.

من به‌انگلیسی گفتم «خوش‌حالم.» و به آن مرد دست دادم، و دیگر چیزی نداشتم که بگویم. ساکت نشستم، مانند دیگران، تا ببینم چه پیش می‌آید، و می‌دیدم چه پرت بود که از کارم بی‌کارم کرده‌اند آورده‌اندم از خانه‌ام این‌جا که حالا ندانم به جز سکوت چه باید کرد. دیدم نمی‌شود نشست همین‌جوری و چیزی نگفت، گفتم «گفتند شعر می‌گویید.»

ساده سر جنباند و گفت «همین‌جوره.» جوری گفت که انگار گفته باشد چه‌کار کنم، دیگر.

گفتم «اسمتان توماس است؟» ساده سر جنباند، گفت «همین‌جوره.» گفتم «با شاعری به نام دایلون توماس نسبتی دارید؟»

گفت «دیلن.» تلفظ آن اسم را برایم درست کرده بود. گفت «دیلن تامس. خودم هستم.»

اول یکه‌یی خوردم اما زود ملتفت شدم که چهره‌اش اگرچه بادکرده می‌نمایاند و از تازه‌سالی افتاده است، اما همان چهره است که در عکس‌هایش از او دیده بودم از سال‌های جوان‌تر و کم‌تر آبجوخورده‌اش. من به شعرهایش اول سه سالی پیش در ماه‌نامه‌های هورایزن[1] برخورد کرده بودم و از نزدیکی صدائی و آهنگ کلمه‌های به‌جا و دقیق و اوج‌گیرنده‌شان، وقتی بلند می‌خواندیشان، لذت گرفته بودم از بیان روانِ حس و دیدِ جوینده و معنای برگزیده، و از جَستِ تیروارِ تصور که آسوده‌بودنِ سرعت را به شدتِ کشیده‌بودنِ اعصاب متصل می‌کرد، و تلألؤ کلام را از شتاب و فرزبودن و از ضربت و نوازش و برندگی می‌ساخت، مثل شهاب‌ها در شب. لذت

writing, nor the mere arrangement of words on the page. And as I was standing there among these casual friends, Mr. Abusaidi introduced me to the Englishman, in English, and introduced the Englishman to me, in Persian, saying, "This is Mr. Thomas who apparently writes poetry in England and has now come here to do some studying in preparation for writing a script."

From this "do some studying" it was clear he had said this part in Persian.

"Glad to meet you," I said, in English, and shook the man's hand and then was unable to think of anything further to say. I sat in silence, like the others, waiting to see what would happen next, and I thought how senseless it was that they had dragged me away from my work and brought me here where I didn't know what to do, other than keep silent. After a while it occurred to me that it was not right to just sit there and say nothing, so I said, "They say you write poetry."

He just shook his head and said, "That's right." The way he said it was as if he was saying, What else can I do, after all.

I said, "Your name is Thomas?"

He just moved his head and said, "That's right."

"Are you related to a poet called Dylan Thomas?" I said.

"Dylan," 'he said, correcting my pronunciation. He said, "Dylan Thomas. That is me."

I was taken aback at first but soon realized that his face was still the same face I had seen in photos of him from his younger, less beer-bloated days. I had first encountered his poetry three years earlier, in the *Horizon* monthly magazine, and had enjoyed the synchronicity of their sounds, the rhythm of their well-picked, precise soaring words, particularly when you read them out loud. I had enjoyed their smooth description of sensation and their searching gaze and their measured meanings, and the thunder-like pace that conveyed the speed of the image to the wrought nerves, and from the pace and speed of the poetry, and its thump, and its tenderness and its edge, created a shimmer of

گرفته بودم و در حد خود پیش خود، در شور، او را و آن‌ها را ستوده بودم چندان که از چندتائی‌شان چند سطری از برم بودم. اکنون از این‌که، غافلگیر و ازپیش‌ندانسته، می‌دیدم خودش روبه‌روی من نشسته بود یکه خورده بودم و او را نگاه می‌کردم، نگاه می‌کردم که ناگهان از خودم شنیدم به انگلیسی بلند می‌خوانم:

«دستی که بر سند امضا گذاشت شهری را فرو انداخت
«پنج انگشتِ خودمختار راه نفس را بست
«کرهٔ مرگ را مضاعف کرد و کشوری را دوباره
«این پنج شاه شاهی را از پا درآوردند...»

اکنون او بود که یکه خورده مرا با چشم‌های ثاقب از درخشش پرسش‌های ناشناخته می‌پایید. در چشم‌هایش هرچه را که می‌شد خواست می‌شد دید. نمی‌دانستم خودش چه می‌خواهد و از این شعر از او خواندن چه برداشت‌ها دارد. نگاهش مرا پشیمان کرد. گفتم «عذر می‌خواهم.» عذر از چه می‌خواستم؟ از این‌که با شعرش در جایی غریبه غافلگیر کرده بودمش؟ می‌دانستم که شعرهای بهتری دارد، و بعضی‌هاشان را هم به یاد داشتم اما نمی‌دانستم چرا این یکی به ذهن و زبانم رسیده بود؛ شاید از این تصور سرپائی که در این یکی بیان او به برداشت‌های سیاسی‌ام جور می‌آمد. تعجب و غافل‌گرفتگی شاید همراه با نوعی رضایت و شاید با نوعی دل‌آزردگی در نگاهش بود، که زود و آهسته، نرم، مبدل شد به پذیرفتن چیزی که واقع بود، چیزی که بی‌ضرر، و حتی شاید مغتنم، هم بود. در این میان صدای حالت را شنیدم که چیزی گفت که من نفهمیدم و همکارانم به خنده افتادن. پرسیدم از چه می‌خندند. جواب جمعشان خنده بود، دوباره. گفتم «بچه‌ها

words, like shooting stars. And I had, in my own mind, and with my own kind of exhilaration, so appreciated him and his poems, and had so enjoyed them, that I knew a few lines by heart. It took me by surprise that now, with no advance warning, while I was looking at him as he sat across from me, I suddenly heard myself recite loudly, in English:

> The hand that signed the paper felled a city;
> Five sovereign fingers taxed the breadth,
> Doubled the globe of dead and halved a country;
> These five kings did a king to death.[6]

Now it was his turn to be taken aback, and he began examining me, his eyes alight with unanswered questions. In his eyes, you could see anything you wanted. I did not know what he wanted, and what he thought about my recitation of his poem. His expression made me regret what I had done. I said, "I apologize." What was I apologizing for? That I had, with his poetry, surprised him in a strange land? I knew he had written better poems, some of which I knew by heart, but I did not know why this one had come to mind and rolled off my tongue. Maybe because of the flimsy notion that the language of this poem better fit my own political persuasions. Surprise, and a sense of being taken aback, maybe a touch of gratification, and possibly even also a sense of hurt, were all evident in his expression, but quickly, calmly, and softly, it seemed to turn into acceptance of the situation in which he found himself as benign, maybe even auspicious. Meanwhile, I heard Halat saying something that I didn't catch but which made my colleagues laugh. I asked what they were laughing about and their collective response was more laughter, again. I said, "Guys, it is not right to laugh; this fellow

---

6. You can hear this poem, "The hand that signed the paper," written in 1935, recited by Richard Burton, https://www.youtube.com/watch?v=wHfVpuE6szM.

درست نیست خندیدن. بابا ممکنه فکر کنه چیزی که گفته‌اید برای مسخره‌ش‌کردن بود، به او هس که می‌خندین.»

آقای ابوسعیدی که کارش فقط احتیاط‌کردن، و سهمش در آن خنده‌ها یك شبه‌تبسم کم‌عرض بود گفت، و به‌انگلیسی گفت، و آقای حالت که از سرشناس‌ترین شاعران ایران‌اند می‌گویند این آقای گلستان تا امروز ما را قبول نمی‌کرد و هی شاعری به اسم نیما را می‌کوفت توی کله‌مان، حالا به‌کل شده است طرفدارغربی‌ها.

من یقین دارم حالت نگفته بود غربی‌ها، و اگر گفته بود چیزی در این حدود اصلاً، گفته بوده فرنگی‌ها، اگر نه خاجپرست‌ها؛ اما هم احتیاط و هم احترام و هم نبودن یك کلمهٔ کاملاً دقیق و دم‌دست و عیناً و آماده در زبان انگلیسی برای فرنگی، آقای ابوسعیدی را به چنین انتخاب و ترجمه آورده بود تا در مهمان اثر نامناسبی نگذاشته باشد. و پیدا بود که در فکر میهمان، خودش، نه نیمائی بود نه ابوالقاسم حالتی، و نه او اصلاً خبر از این‌ها داشت. میهمان در عوالم دیگر بود. میهمان شاید الان درست نمی‌دانست حالا در کدام گوشهٔ دنیا نشسته است، تشنه است، گرمش است. شاید هم شوقش از این‌که در چنین برهوت غریبه‌یی کسی به شعر او آشنا بوده است اکنون تکیده بود. درهرحال، ساکت بود. در عوالم دیگر بود. کاری به کار چنین قصه‌ها نداشت اگر اصلاً کاری به کار مردم بیگانه و این‌جور جزئیات مردمِ حتی محیط اصلیِ خود و حتی خود محیط اصلی خود داشت. که من گمان نمی‌کنم هم داشت. آقای ابوسعیدی برای ختم غائله، که از اصل غائله‌یی هم نبود، یا برای پیشگیری از وقوع وضع محتمل نامناسب‌تر نگاه به ساعت کرد و به‌انگلیسی گفت «خب وقت ناهار هم شد.»

might think you said something to make fun of him, that you are laughing at him."

Mr. Abusaidi, who always erred on the side of caution, and whose contribution to the laughter was but a tight-lipped half-grin, commented, in English, that Mr. Halat was one of Iran's most renowned poets and that he had been saying that Mr. Golestan here never took us seriously, always scorning us by shoving a poet called Nima down our throats, but now, it seemed, he had suddenly become a fan of Westerners.

I am certain Halat had not said "Westerners," and even if he had said anything remotely like it, he might have used the word *farangi*[7], if not the cross-worshipers. But caution, and respect, and the absence of a reliable and precise equivalent for the word *farangi*, had forced Mr. Abusaidi to pick such an equivalent, lest another word might elicit an unintended response; it was clear, though, that neither Nima nor Abolgassam Halat had any place in the mind of the guest, and indeed he did not know anything about either of them. The guest was in another world. He might not at that moment have known what corner of the world he was in, or was he thirsty, or hot. Maybe the joy of discovering, in this strange barren land, someone who was familiar with his poetry had already dissipated. In any case, he was silent. He was in a strange world and uninterested in these tales, if indeed he was interested in the strange people around him or the details of their lives; or if he was even interested in details of the lives of people in his own country, or even at home, in his surroundings. And I did not think he was. To end the awkwardness, which might not have been present at first, or maybe to prevent an even more uncomfortable situation, he looked at the clock and said in English, "Well, it must be time for lunch."

---

7. From the time of the Crusades, a common name given to
   Westerners was *farangi*—a derivative of the Franks. In modern
   Persian usage, *farangi* generally doesn't have a negative
   connotation.

دلک‌کردن بود نه اعلام وقت، اما دلک‌کردنی به‌دقت بود که همکاران را از دورهم‌نشستن بی‌تکلیف، از دورهم‌نشستن بی‌ربط به موضوع و علت این دورهم‌نشستن رها می‌کرد. جنبیدند به ازجابلندشدن. آقای ابوسعیدی به‌احتیاط و تا لبهٔ زبر حرف را نرم کرده باشد رفت توی این توضیح که وقت قطع کار روز برای نهار کارمندان پالشگاه در بخش‌های صنعتی نیم‌ساعت زودتر از وقت بخش‌های اداری است، و این تفاوت وقت دو دسته کارمند برای بیش‌تر بهره‌بردن از کم‌تر وسیله‌های رفت‌وآمد است — توضیحی که کمابیش ربطی نداشت به احوال و کار و کنج‌کاوی مرد غریبه‌یی که آن‌جا بود و این برایش بود، و اکنون برخاسته بود بهرفتن چون می‌دید که همکاران در این میان با سرتکان‌دادن یکی‌یکی رفتند. آقای ابوسعیدی که ایستاده بود پشت میزش به او می‌گفت اگرچه تا مهمان‌سرای شرکت که لابد نهار را در آن‌جا خواهد خورد راهی نیست اما اتومبیلی هست که او را ببرد آن‌جا، و پرسید می‌خواهد؟

من از او سئوال کردم یا میل دارد نهار با هم باشیم. بی‌تکلف و مکثی قبول کرد.

حرف‌های ابوسعیدی و رفتار همکاران بیگانه‌بودن و تنهائی او را برای من آسیب‌پذیرتر نشان می‌داد اما نمی‌خواستم خیال کند من کشیده می‌شوم، یا شدم، به شهرت و نامش. شهرتش فراوان نبود آن‌روز، چون نمرده بود هنوز، آن هم از مستی. کنج‌کاوی‌هایم فراوان بود، اما عوامل منع سئوال و کنج‌کاوی هم فراوان بود، که از تماشمان تواناتر شعرش. شعرش صریح بود و پر از شور بود و زیر سطح درخشان پر از جرقه و تلاطم بود. ظرفیت و توانِ گُربرداشتن داشت. حرمت به گوهر شعرش مرا می‌کشاند، و همان هم به درک آسیب‌پذیریش، به خود آسیب‌پذیریش، و این درک بود مایهٔ منع من از سئوال — که بر چنان منع از سئوال می‌افزود. پیاده راه افتادیم.

This was a careful signal that my colleagues should cut out, not an announcement of time, and it freed them from an aimless gathering, from a senseless meeting that had nothing to do with their job. They moved to get up. As a precaution, and to soften any sharp edges in the conversation, Mr. Abusaidi went into some detail about how the lunch break for the dayshift of the refinery's industrial staff was half an hour earlier than the break for the office staff, adding that the different lunch hours for the two groups of employees was to make best use of the limited transport available, mundane explanations that had no real relevance to the mood of the gathering, or the nature of the work or interests of the stranger, for whom the gathering had been arranged, and he had gotten up to leave on seeing that my colleagues were departing, one by one, each nodding their head to him as they left. Mr. Abusaidi, standing behind his desk, was now telling the stranger that although the distance to the company guest house, where he would probably be having lunch, was not far, there was a company car that could take him there, and he asked if he wanted a lift.

I asked him whether he would like to have lunch with me. Without affectation or hesitation, he accepted. The words of Abusaidi and the behavior of my colleagues served only to emphasize his state of isolation and abandonment, in my view. I did not want him to think that I was drawn, or could be drawn, to him merely by his fame or reputation. His fame was still not that great in those days. Because he hadn't yet died, and nor from drink either. My curiosity was strong, but factors inhibiting my curiosity and the desire to question him were equally strong, the strongest being my admiration for his poetry. His poetry was frank, and full of vigor, and under its bright sheen it was full of sparks and tumult. It had the capacity and power to ignite. Respect for the quality of his poetry enticed me, and the same respect helped me understand his vulnerability, both as a poet and as a person, and this recognition was itself preventing me from asking questions, adding to my feeling of inhibition. We started walking.

رستوران دور نبود از اداره. در ماه‌های غیرداغ سال خوشایند بود ازلای‌نخل‌هارفتن. گفتم راهمان زیاد نیست. پرنده‌هایی که به‌شان بلبل خرمائی می‌گفتند آواز می‌خواندند. بوی خوش بهار از گل‌های یونجه که لای چمن درآمده بودند می‌رسید. گل‌های یونجه یا چیزی شبیه‌شان میان چمن‌های به گرما و باد و خاكِ شور خوکرده درمی‌آمدند و به نخلستان و محلّهٔ آن بوی خوشایند می‌دادند. می‌رفتیم و او ساکت بود. نمی‌دانستم این سکوت از حجب است یا خودش خسته است یا چیزی برای گفتن نمی‌بیند. نمی‌دانستم این برای او عادی است یا دارد تحمیل می‌کند به خود به خاطر این پرت‌افتادن. می‌دیدم هر حرف پرت را می‌شود برای بازکردن صحبت به کار آورد اما انگار هیچ فرقی نبود یا من نمی‌دیدم میان هیچ‌نگفتن با گفت‌وگوی آن‌جوری. آخر گفتم «این‌جا تمام خانه‌ها و سیستم آمدشد و آب و خوراك و ورزش و تفریح، تمام در دست شرکت است. مال شرکت است.»

سر جنباند.

گفتم «این رستوران که می‌رویم هم مال شرکت است فقط نمی‌دانم چه‌جور معماریش را داده بوده‌اند، گویا، به ارشیتکت‌های آلمانی. پیش از جنگ. این خانه هم که می‌بینید، انگار انبار، این‌ها هم "نیسن هت"های زمان جنگ بوده‌اند برای خانهٔ خلبان‌ها و افسران مأمور دفاع از پالشگاه.»

سر جنباند.

گفتم «در این جزیره — چون آبادان یك جزیرهٔ دلتائی است میان دو رود و آخرش دریا، خلیج — در این جزیره جز خود خاك جزیره هرچه هست و می‌بینید با صنعت شروع شد و پیش از آن چیزی نبود، ساکنی نداشت. فقط، هزار سال پیش، یك شاعر بزرگ ما گذشت از این‌جا و در تمام این جزیره فقط برخورد به یك عابد تنهای منزوی، فقط. تنها.»

The restaurant was not far from the office. In the not sizzling months of the year, it was pleasant to walk beneath the palm trees. I said we don't have far to go. Birds known as date parrots were singing. The sweet smell of spring wafted from the alfalfa flowers blooming in the grass. Having become acclimatized to the heat and the wind and the salty earth, the alfalfa flowers, or what appeared to be alfalfa flowers, filled the palm grove and the whole neighborhood with a pleasant aroma. As we walked, my companion remained silent. I did not know whether his silence was from shyness, or whether he was simply tired or thought there nothing worth talking about. I didn't know whether this was normal for him or whether he was forcing it on himself, given his current disorientation. It seemed that I could say any old nonsense to initiate a conversation and it made no difference, or at least I could see no difference between saying nothing and making that kind of conversation. Finally I said, "Here everything —from the housing and transport to the water and food and sports and entertainment—is in the hands of the company. They all are owned by the company."

He shook his head.

I said, "The restaurant we are going to also belongs to the company. I've no idea why they had, apparently, commissioned German architects to design it. Before the war. These buildings you see, that look like storage units, were wartime Nissen huts. To house the pilots and officers assigned to defend the refinery."

He shook his head.

I said, "On this island—since Abadan is an island in the delta between two rivers and at the end there is the sea, the [Persian] Gulf, this island, in its entirety and everything you can see, save for its earth, was set up by industry; before it there was nothing, and no inhabitants. A thousand years ago, one of our great poets passed by this place, and in this entire island he encountered only one pious, solitary man. Only one person. All alone."

می‌دانستم تمام حرف‌هایم زیادی است اما نمی‌شد فقط خاموش رفت،
که این می‌شد یک‌جور بی‌اعتنائی، تأکید این‌که او غریبه است.

پرسید «هزار سال پیش؟»

گفتم «هزار سال پیش.»

«شاعر بود؟»

«فیلسوف هم بود. جهان‌گرد هم بود. فرستادهٔ مذهبی، مبلغ هم بود.»

باز پرسید «شاعر بود؟»

«آره.»

«یعنی که شعر می‌گفت و می‌نوشت؟»

«آره. پس چی؟»

«در چه زبانی؟»

«همین زبان ما. همین زبان که بهش حرف می‌زنیم این‌جا. همین زبان
که فارسی است اسمش.»

«می‌شود خواندش؟ شعرش را؟»

«چرا که نه؟»

«هزار سال پیش؟»

«هزار سال پیش. زبان محکمی هم بود. هنوز هم می‌شود
باشد. می‌شود آن را درست و کاملاً فهمید. فرقی نکرده زبان، خیلی. ما
مثل مومیائی سفتیم.» و خنده‌یی کردم. گفتم «سفتیم، که هم‌چنان
هنوز هم هستیم و می‌فهمیم، تاحدی‌که ممکن‌مان است می‌فهمیم. یا
فهم‌مان مومیائی شده است که هم‌چنان هنوز همان‌جور می‌فهمیم وقتی
که می‌فهمیم، اگر که بفهمیم، البته. یا هم‌چنان هنوز فکر می‌کنیم که
می‌فهمیم.»

به این وصف حال امروزمان که من کردم توجهی نکرد، و هم‌چنان
هنوز، انگار، در بند فکر کهنه‌بودنمان بود. گفت،

I knew I was chatting for the sake of it, but it was impossible to just walk in silence. It would be construed as a kind of indifference, I felt, or draw attention to his being a stranger.

"A thousand years ago?" he asked.

"A thousand years ago." I said.

"He was a poet?"

"He was also a philosopher. A world traveler, too. A missionary, and a proselytizer."[8]

Again, he asked, "He was a poet?"

"Yes."

"Meaning he composed and wrote poetry?"

"Yes, what else?"

"In what language did he write?"

"In our own language, in the language that we speak here. The same language that is called Persian."

"Can one still read it? His poems?"

"Why not?"

"Poetry written a thousand years ago?"

"A thousand years ago, it was even then a fully developed language. It still is. It can be understood clearly and completely. The language hasn't changed much. We are like mummies, resilient." And I smiled. I went on, "We are resilient and that is why we are still here, and we still understand, as much as it is possible for us to understand, we understand. Either our understanding has been mummified, so we still understand the same way, if we understand. Or we just think we still understand."

To my description of our condition today, he paid no attention, being still apparently stuck on the idea of our being timeworn.

---

8. Golestan is referring to Nasser Khosrow (1004-1088). His poetry and travel writings are considered classics of Persian letters. He proselytized in favor of the Ismaili version of Shiism, a group known for their bravery in battle and rationalism in matters of faith.

«هزار سال پیش!»

«پیش‌تر از او هم هست. بهتر از او پیش‌تر از او هم هست.»

«در همان زبان؟»

«در همین زبان.» داشت به‌ام برمی‌خورد از این‌که نمی‌داند، و ندانستنش حالا به صورت باورنکردنش درآمده است، انگار.

باز گفت «هزار سال!»

گفتم «می‌شه چندین قرن پیش‌تر از چاسر، می‌شه درواقع حدود دورهٔ ویلیام فاتح، و جنگ هیستینگز.»

آرام و فارغ نگاهم کرد. دیدم زیاده رفته‌ام. گفتم «قصد ملیت‌نمائی نداشتم، می‌بخشید.» نداشتم هم، درواقع، به‌راستی. قصدم تنها معیاردادن بود. قیاس بود جوری‌که برایش شناختنی باشد. بی‌قصد و فکرِ پیش بود و خودش نشد کرده بود و حرف حرف آورده بود، فقط. تصادف بود. تصادف هم حالا کمک می‌داد ــ به حرف عوض‌کردن. رسیده بودیم به رستوران، در ساختمانی که به‌اش «انکس» می‌گفتند. گفتم «این‌جا را بهش انکس می‌گن. چون اضافه‌اش کرده‌اند به آن ساختمان، که "جیم ـ خانه"س.» و جیم‌خانه را ساختمانی به سبک مستعمراتی هندی بود به‌اش نشان دادم اما نخواستم به‌اش بگویم که تا همین چند سال پیش ورود سگ و ایرانی به آن ممنوع بوده است. درعوض گفتم «جیم‌خانه یک لغت کج‌وکوله‌شدهٔ دراصل ایرانی و هندی است که از جمع‌خانه می‌آید. به معنی کلوب، جای جمع‌شدن، دورهم‌بودن.»

رفتیم تو. تو، مثل هفت ـ هشت ماه از سال از همان دم از هوا خنک می‌شد. اما بوی ماندهٔ آب‌جوخوردن‌ها و سیگارکشیدن‌ها همیشه می‌آمد. بالا که می‌رفتیم از پله‌های‌ساختمان گفتم «رستوران بالاست.»

گفت «من تشنه‌م. این‌جا بار هم هست؟»

He said, "A thousand years ago?"

"There are those who even precede him, better than him, and who came before him."

"Writing in the same language?"

"In the same language." I was beginning to feel insulted, that he did not know, and his ignorance appeared now to have turned into disbelief.

Again he said, "A thousand years?"

I said, "That makes it a few centuries before Chaucer, around the time of William the Conqueror and the Battle of Hasting."

Calmly and nonchalantly, he looked at me. I saw that I had gone too far. I said, "I wasn't trying to play patriotic. Forgive me." I truly and honestly hadn't been playing that game. My sole purpose had been to offer some measure for comparison. A comparison to aid comprehension. It was with no malice forethought, it had simply slipped out, and one thing had led to another. It was an accident. And fate was intervening again, this time to lend a hand—something to change the conversation. We had arrived at the restaurant, in a building called the Annex. I said, "They call this place the Annex. Because it has been added to that building called the Jam Khaneh." And I showed him the Jam Khaneh, built in Indian colonial style, and I did not want to tell him that, up until a few years ago, dogs and Iranians were barred from entering the place. Instead I said, "*Jam khaneh* is a mangled term, a mixture of Persian and Indian in origin, and it comes from the plural for a house. Meaning a club. A place to gather, a place to be together."

We went inside. For about seven to eight months of the year, it was cool inside, right from the hallway. But there was also always the stale smell of consumed beer and smoked cigarettes. As we climbed the stairs, I said, "The restaurant is on the upper floor."

He said, "I'm thirsty. Is there a bar here?"

گفتم «تمام این درازای ایوان بالای پله‌ها بار است. درواقع دو تا بار است، در دو دست سر پله ــ ازبس که مشتری فراوان است.»

رفتیم توی تالار بارها. یک انتهای فضا را به او نشان دادم گفتم «آن‌جا در باز می‌شود به کتاب‌خانه و محل خواندن کتاب، که هرچه در انگلستان کتاب چاپ می‌شود، علی‌الخصوص از قصه و تاریخ و جنگ و جهان‌گردی، و البته در بارۀ سگ و گل و کریکت، یک نسخه می‌خرند می‌فرستند به این‌جا. آن‌ور هم تالارهای پینگ‌پُنگ و بیلیارد و ورق‌بازی است. وسط هم که می‌رود به تالار رستوران. این‌ها هم دو تا بار، پر از هرجور نوشیدنی به جز شراب. شما انگلیسی‌ها شراب دوست نمی‌دارین.»

گفت «من اهل ولز هستم.»

از تصحیح‌کردنش فکر کردم که به‌اش برخورد انگلیسی‌اش گفتم. فکر کردم تمام توضیحات که در بارۀ بنا و باشگاه و بار داده بودم و پرحرفی بود تنها برای پاک‌کردن اثر آن قیاس میان زمان ناصرخسرو و هجوم و فتح انگلستان به دست نرمان‌ها، که برخورده بود به‌اش، شاید، ورپرید از میانه و حالا از این‌که به او گفته‌ام شما انگلیسی‌ها دوباره به‌اش برخورد. وادادم، گفتم «می‌خواستم بگویم شمای انگلیسی‌زبان» درهرحال زبان که انگلیسی بود. بار از انبوه مشتری‌های ظهر خالی می‌شد. ما جای خلوت‌تری گیر آوردیم و لم دادیم.

گفت «از خیلی قدیم بهترین شراب‌های فرانسه را اشراف انگلیسی می‌آوردند، حتی دانشگاه‌های آکسفورد و کمبریج که هنوز هم می‌آورند. اصلاً چندین واحد شراب‌سازی فرانسه مال انگلیسی‌هاست. حتی اسم شراب‌ها که بعضی‌شان به اسم صاحبان انگلیسی تاکستان‌ها و شراب‌اندازی‌هاست.»

این یک‌جور تصحیح دیگر بود. گفتم «شراب خوب منحصر به فرانسه نیست. فرانسه معروف است.»

گفت «اسپانیا؟ ایتالیا؟»

گفتم «از ترانس اوکسانی و شمال شرقی ایران در شعرهای ما تعریف شرابشان فراوان است.» «ماوراء جیحون» را به اسم غربیش ترانس اوکسانی گفتم. و گفتم «من خودم به تجربۀ شخصی‌ام شراب گرجستان را چشیده‌ام

I said, "There is a bar that runs the full length of the hall at the top of the stairs. In fact, there are two bars, one on each side of the staircase—since there are so many customers."

We entered the hall leading to the bars. Showing him one end of the hall, I said, "There the door opens to the library and the reading room, and a copy of every book that is published in England—especially fiction and books on history and war and world travel, and of course on dogs and flowers and cricket—is bought and sent here. On the other side is the room for ping pong, billiards, and card games. And through the door in the middle you enter the restaurant. And here are the two bars, full of every kind of libation, save wine. You English don't like wine."

He said, "I am from Wales."

From the way he had corrected me, I assumed he was insulted that I had called him English. I had hoped all my explanations about the building and the club and the bar might have erased what he had thought was my offence in comparing Naser Khosrow with the Norman invasion and the conquest of England, and maybe all that chatter had helped assuage his hurt feelings, but now he was again offended because I had called him an Englishman. I gave up. I said, "I wanted to say, you English-speaking people." The language was, after all, English. The bar was emptying of its noon crowd. We found a quiet corner and collapsed.

He said, "From way back, the best French wines were brought over by British aristocrats, and Oxford and Cambridge universities still do. In fact, a few French wineries are owned by the British. Even some of the wines are named after the British owners of the wineries and vineyards."

This was yet another form of correction. I said, "Good wine is not limited to France. France is just famous for it."

He said, "Spain? Italy?"

"There is much praise in our poetry for the wines from Transoxiana and the northwest of Iran," I said, using the older name Transoxiana for Amu-Darya. "I myself have tasted a Georgian

که راستی روی ذائقه می‌رقصد. ولی به‌هرصورت این‌ها کجا می‌شود شیراز؟»

«شیراز؟»

«شیراز، شراب خلّر شیراز.»

«کجاست این شیراز؟»

گفتم «آن‌جا که اسم شهر خرز در اندلس را می‌گویند بنی‌امیه‌یی‌های اندلس از آن گرفته‌اند چون، می‌گویند، سرمشق و پایهٔ شراب‌سازی آن محصول شهر ما بوده است.»

گفت «کجاست این شیراز؟»

گفتم «زیاد دور نیست از این‌جا ــ بر حسب کیلومتر، به پرواز پرنده، به خط مستقیم.»

خدمتکار بار آمد بپرسد چه می‌خواهیم. او آبجو می‌خواست من سفارش «مک ایوون» دادم که آبجو از جوِ برشته است و از اسکاتلند می‌آوردند و رنگ قهوه‌ئی دارد. او در فکر فرو رفته بود ولی دیگر آن چهرهٔ ولِ از دلمردگیِ بی‌تکلیفِ توی اتاق اداره را نداشت. پرسید «در کدام کشور؟»

گفتم «در همین کشور.»

گفت «همین پرشیا؟»

گفتم «درواقع شیراز مرکز امروزی پرشیای اصلی تاریخ هرودوت و یونانی‌ها‌س. جغرافیائی زیاد دور نیست از این‌جا، تاریخی چرا. بر حسب وقت روز ــ خیلی زیاد.»

خدمتکار بار آبجو را آورد. جَلد آورده بود. مشتری‌های بار کم شده بودند و وقت نوبت کارش به سر می‌رسید و موقع رفتن به خانه بود برایش. او لیوان بلند آبجوش را برداشت، کمی مزه کرد و بعد جرعه‌یی نوشید. پرسید «حملهٔ نرمان‌ها چه سالی بود؟»

از لحنش پیدا بود برای امتحان من نمی‌پرسد. می‌پرسد. فکری کردم اما سال را درست به یاد نیاوردم. گفتم «گمان می‌کنم ۱۰۶۶ یا شاید ۱۰۴۴ یا شاید چیزی در این حدود.»

wine that truly danced on the palate. But none of these places is a match for Shiraz?" I continued.

"Shiraz?"

"Shiraz, Shiraz's *Kholar* wine."

"Where is this Shiraz?"

"It is the place after which the city of Alcazar in Andalusia, built by the Andalusian Bani Umayyah, is said to have been named, because their model and style of winemaking had come from our city."

"Where is this Shiraz?" he said.

I said, "Not far from here. In kilometers, as the bird flies, a direct line."

The waiter had come to take our order. My companion wanted beer. I ordered a McEwan's, which is brewed from toasted barley, imported from Scotland, and brown in color. He was deep in thought but that look of languid resignation to the boredom of ambivalence that had crept on to his face in the office was no longer there. "In what country is Shiraz?" he asked.

"In this country." I said.

"The same Persia as today?" he said.

I said, "In reality today's Shiraz was the capital of the Persia in the time of Herodotus's *Histories* and for the Greeks. Geographically, it isn't far from here; historically it is. In those times, very far away."

The waiter had brought the beer. He had brought it quickly. There were fewer customers, and his shift was ending and it was time for him to go home. My companion picked up his tall beer glass, took a sip, and then took a gulp. He asked, "The Norman invasion was in what year?"

From his tone, it was clear he wasn't testing me. He was just asking. I thought a bit, but could not remember the precise year. I said, "I think it was 1066, or maybe 1044 or sometime around then."

پاهایش را جفت‌هم دراز کرده بود و دست‌هایش را گذاشته بود روی شکم. این بار پرسید «تاریخ چاسر چه وقت بود؟»

آن را هم اصلاً به یاد نیاوردم. اصلاً تقریباً حتماً از تاریخ تولد یا مرگ او بی‌خبر بودم. چیزی هم از چاسر نخوانده بودم، فقط می‌دانستم که او بوده است و آنچه را هم که از او دیده بودم به زبان انگلیسی امروز درست جور درنمی‌آمد. باز هم حس کردم برای آزمایش من نیست که می‌پرسد. فقط ساده می‌پرسد. گفتم «یک دویست ـ سیصدسالی بعد از مرگ حافظ بود.»

«مرگ کی؟»

«حافظ.»

«حافظ؟»

«شاعرترین شاعرها، آن‌قدر شاعر که ما به او می‌گوییم زبان دنیای نادیده.»

«نشنیده بودم من.»

پیش خودم گفتم اسم‌شنیدن ربط ندارد به شناسائی.

پرسید «کجائی بود؟»

«شیرازی. همان شیراز.»

«و از آن شراب‌ها می‌خورد؟» رندی در سئوال و لحنش بود.

گفتم «شاید لاینقطع.»

«آن‌قدر؟ مسلمان نبود مگر؟»

He had by then spread his two tightly joined legs and placed one hand on his stomach. Then he asked, "When was Chaucer's time?"

That one I also could not remember. In fact, I am almost certain that I knew nothing about his date of birth or death. I hadn't read any Chaucer. I knew only that he existed, and whatever I had read of his work did not much correspond to present-day English language. I again did not think that my companion was trying to test me. He was simply asking a question. I hazarded, "About two to three hundred years after the death of Hafez."[9]

"The death of who?"

"Hafez."

"Hafez?"

"The most poetic of all poets, so much a poet that we call him the voice of the unseen world."

"I haven't heard of him."

I reminded myself that having heard of someone is no proof of knowing that person.

He asked, "Where was he from?

"From Shiraz. The same Shiraz."

"And he drank those wines?" There was something of the *rend*[10] in his question and tone.

I said, "Maybe constantly."

"That much? Wasn't he a Muslim?"

---

9. Chaucer, 1340–1400; Hafez, 1325–90.
10. Hafez's *rend* is a composite of the Perfect Man of gnostic Sufism, the impoverished beggar in the road, the libertine, and the political rebel who refuses to bow. See Encyclopædia Iranica, online edition, https://iranicaonline.org/articles/hafez-viii.

«قرآن را از بر می‌خواند، با چهارده روایت. اصلاً اسمش یعنی کسی که قرآن را تمام از حفظه. کاری هم هست، ها!»

«آن‌وقت این‌جور هم لاینقطع می‌خورد؟»

گفتم «لاینقطع که چندان نه، شاید. خوردن که می‌خورده. بی‌دریغ می‌خورده. گفته که گاهی هم گیرش نمی‌اومده، گاهی. که من باور نمی‌کنم. درهرحال وقتی هم گیرش نمی‌اومده، خودش می‌گه از ته‌نشین‌های توی خمره می‌خورده.»

«خمره؟»

«که توش شراب می‌اندازن.»

«خمره؟»

فهمیدم چرا تعجب کرد. گفتم «ما این‌جا چلیك نداریم. این‌جا تو خمره شراب می‌اندازن.»

«جالبه.»

«بوی بلوط و طعمش را نمی‌گیره، البته، اما محفوظه از گرما. رسم نیس از بلوط بشكه بسازن. نمی‌سازیم. بلوط كم داریم. اگر اصلاً. خاك رس بسیار. ما از خاكیم در خلقت. مگر نه؟»

«جالبه.»

«هرچیز از خاكه، هركجا این‌جا. سفر كنی این‌جا، می‌بینی خونه‌ها از گِل‌ان همه، بیش‌تر. یك باریكه‌جنگل كنار بحر خزر بقیه همه‌ش صحرا و سنگ و كوهستان. ساختن با گِل آسون‌تره تا سنگ. با این‌كه كوه فراوونه. همینه كه از روزگار اسكندر به این طرف خونه‌یی، قصری، معبدی از سنگ نیس این‌جا. همه‌ش از گِل. پخته یا نپخته همه‌ش از گِل. می‌آییم و می‌رویم و چه‌چیزی باقی بمونه رفته‌ایم دیگه، به ما چه مربوطه. اینه. اینیم.»

"He knew the Qur'an by heart. In fourteen different iterations. Even his name means someone who knows the entire Qur'an by heart. A big deal, no?"

"Nevertheless, he still drank constantly?"

I said, "Constantly, maybe not quite. Drinking he no doubt did. He drank with abandon. He even claimed sometimes that he couldn't find anything to drink. Sometimes. Which personally I don't believe. Anyway, he said that, when he couldn't find any, he would drink the dregs at the bottom of the clay barrel."

"Clay barrel?"

"The barrel in which the wine was made."

"A clay barrel?"

Realizing why he was surprised, I said, "Here we don't have wooden barrels. We used clay barrels to make wine."

"That's interesting."

"A clay barrel won't have the aroma and flavor of oak, of course. But it keeps the wine safe from the heat. It is not the custom to make barrels from oak here, so we don't make them. We have little, if any oak, but lots of red clay. We are all created from the earth, are we not?"

"That's interesting."

"Everything is made from the earth here. Everywhere you look. If you travel here, you'll see. The houses are all made of clay, or most of them are. We have a small slither of forest near the Caspian Sea, and the rest is all desert and boulders and mountains. It is easier to build with clay than with stone, though there are plenty of mountains. That is why since Alexander's time there have been no houses, palaces, or temples made of stone here. All made of clay. All buildings here are made of clay, baked or unbaked. We come and we go, and what is left when we go is of no concern to us, as we have already departed. That is it. That's how we are."

«جالبه.» چشم‌های براقش نشان می‌داد فقط از ادب نیست که می‌گوید.

گفتم «همون حافظ می‌گه زمین بساط و در و دشت بارگاه من است. می‌گه آسمان کلاه من است.» این‌ها را به‌ترجمه گفتم، و ترجمهٔ تند انگلیسی‌ام البته کج‌وکوله بود و بدتر بود از آن‌که اگر وقت و دقت بود. گفتم «عذر می‌خوام شکسته و پس‌وپیش و غیرشعری شد.»

سری جنباند و گفت «مهم نیس.» دلداری‌م می‌داد.

گفتم «در شعرهاش وسعت عمیقی هس. بعضی‌وقتا چنان زیاد که بیرونه از فهم اول و عادی بی آن‌که جمله‌هاش مشکل و پیچیده‌شکل باشن. معنی‌هاش پیچیده‌ن اما درعین‌حال شفاف و نرم به چشم می‌آن. زبون چنون روون که فکر می‌کنن فهمیده‌ن، ولیکن نه. بپرسی چه گفته بود گیر می‌کنن در جواب.»

گفت «جالبه.» و کمی در سکوت گذشت تا پرسید «این‌ها را به زبون دیگری هم درآورده‌ن؟»

بی هیچ فکر گفتم «ممکنه؟ می‌شه؟»

نگاهم کرد. فکر کردم انگار می‌خواست بگوید نفهمیده است چه گفتم. باور نمی‌کردم که نفهمیده باشد. فکر می‌کردم چه بگویم که در جواب تند ناگهانی‌ام اگر نشانه‌یی از قصد نیش‌زدن — که هیچ نداشتم — شناخته باشد اثرش را چه‌جور پاک کنم، چه‌جور بگویم تا حرفم را درست بفهمم. بهاش بگویم که این، همین، آیا خودش نمونهٔ دشواربودن نقل از یك زبان به یك زبان دیگر نیست؟ نشانهٔ آن بار چندپهلوی عاطفی که کلمه در یك زبان دارد و با درآمدن از رنگ و وزن و سابقه‌های روانی و آهنگ آن

"That's interesting." His gleaming eyes indicated he wasn't saying this just out of politeness.

I said, "That same Hafez says that the earth is 'my domain, and my plain and my palace.' He says the sky is 'my hat.'" These words of Hafez I said in English, and of course my off-the-cuff translation was mangled and worse than it would've been if I'd had more time to think.

I said, "I am sorry if that was rough and muddled and unpoetic."

He shook his head and said, "It doesn't matter." He was appeasing me.

I said, "In his poetry there is a vast depth. Sometimes so much that it is beyond initial or easy comprehension, without the lines ever being complicated or convoluted. Their sense is complex but at the same time they seem translucent and easy. Language that is so so effortless that people think they comprehend it, but they don't. If you ask them what did Hafez say, they will have a hard time coming up with an answer."

He said, "That's interesting." And then came a moment of silence before he asked, "Have these been translated into another language?"

Without thinking, I said, "Could they—would it be possible?"

He looked at me. I had the impression he wanted to say he hadn't understood what I'd said. I couldn't believe that he hadn't understood. I wondered what I could say to wash away any suspicion he might have had that my knee-jerk response was meant to make fun of him—which I'd certainly not intended. How could I say it so that he clearly understood what I had meant? Should I say that this in itself, this very misunderstanding, is an example of the difficulty of translating one language into another. Did it not show the nuanced emotional weight that a word has in one language, and how divorced from the color and rhythm and the psychological and musical heritage, how no equivalent word can retain all these nuances in another language? As I had

در آن زبان در زبان دیگری نمی‌آید؟ هنوز چیزی نگفته بودم که بعدِ چندلحظه‌یی
گفت «هرچند با زبونه که شعر برنده‌س.»

در چهره‌اش نشانه‌یی از تیزهوشیِ به من نشان‌دادن و من را به دام آزمایش
و سنجش کشاندنی نمی‌دیدم. شاید من دیدِ تندِ درکِ بازی او را نداشتم، اگر که
بازی بود. یا او در کمال ساده‌بودن و پاکی سئوال کرده بود و پاسخ درست و ساده را
باصفا و درستی اکنون به خود می‌داد.

و گفتم «آره. گوته هم حافظ را خوانده بود، که لابد به آلمانی
بوده. یک ترجمه هم از یک زن به انگلیسی هست که من خوانده‌ام، و حالم را به
هم زده.»

«چرا؟»

«زده، به همان دلیلی که خودتون گفتین.» این خودتانی که من به او گفتم
به خاطر حرمت‌گذاشتن نبود. زبان جاری امروز انگلیسی «تو» را، که قصدم
بود، «شما» می‌کرد.

گفت «انگلیسی؟»

گفتم «بریتانیائی، به‌هرصورت.» تمام کسانی که در انگلستان زندگی می‌کنند
بریتانیائی‌اند اما اهل ولز یا اسکاتلند یا هرجای دیگر دنیا اگر باشند انگلیسی
نمی‌شناسندشان. خودش هم که اهل ولز بود ناچار انگلیسی نبود. یک چند
لحظه پیش هم مرا تصحیح کرده بود و به‌تأکید هرچند نرم، و با غرور محلی،
انگلیسی‌نبودن خود را به من گفته بود.

پرسید «اسمش؟ نه فیتز جرالد؟»

گفتم «گفتم زن. گرترود بل.»

گفت «اوه!» که هم نشانه تصحیح بود هم رنگ تندی از حس‌های منفی
داشت بعد پرسید «مال گوته چه؟»

گفتم «نمی‌دونم. گوته هم لابد ترجمه را خوانده بود. فارسی نمی‌دونسته،
که.»

گفت «اگر تعریف کرده لابد از آن‌چه بوده تعریف می‌کرده، نه از
خود آن شعرها، جوری که شاعر نوشته بوده. بله؟»

still said nothing, after a few moments, he said, "Of course it is in its original language that poetry stings."

In his face I saw no hint that he was trying to show me how clever he was, or that he was trying to trap me into a game of one-upmanship. Maybe I didn't have a sharp enough wit to get his game, if indeed it was a game. Maybe he had asked a question in complete sincerity, and was offering a simple answer, kindly and candidly.

And I said, "Yes. Goethe too had read Hafez, and that was probably in German. There is a translation of it in English by an Englishwoman that I have read, and it turned my stomach."

"Why?"

"It did. For the same reason that you said yourself." The plural honorific "you" I had used was not to show deference. The English vernacular today turns the singular "you" of my intent into the plural "you."

He said, "An English person?"

I said, "British anyway." All who live in England are British but those from Wales or Scotland, or from any other part of the world, are not considered English. He himself, being from Wales, was thus not English. A few minutes earlier he had corrected me, and with emphasis, albeit softly, and with partisan pride, had reminded me he was not English.

"What was his name? Not [Edward] FitzGerald?" he asked.

"I said a woman. Gertrude Bell," I said

He said, "Oh," and the word had a hint of reproof and a sharp edge of hurt feelings, and then he asked, "What about Goethe's?"

"I don't know, but Goethe probably also read Hafez in translation. He didn't know Persian, obviously," I said.

He said, "If he has praised it, he must have praised what was in the poetry, rather than the poems themselves, the way they had been written—yes?"

گفتم «حتماً. نمی‌دونم. شاید. فقط خونده‌م که خیلی خوشش می‌اومده. آن‌قدر که یک مجموعه‌شعرش را به اسم "دیوان شرقی" یا یک همچو چیزی، اسم گذاشته.»

«دیوان؟»

«یعنی مجموعه‌شعر به یک معنی.»

«جالبه. چیزی از آن‌ها در آن‌جا هست؟» و اشاره دستش به آخر تالار بود و کتاب‌خانه که پیش از آن به‌اش گفته بودم و نشان داده بودم به‌اش. کتاب‌خانه خوب و وسیع و بی‌صدا و پرکتابی بود که در آن کتاب را آرام می‌شد خواند و کتاب‌خوانی در آن نمی‌دیدی. سرپرست ایرانی آرام و بی‌صدایی داشت که در جاهای دیگر آن شهر، مانند محل‌های ورزش و تنیس و شنا، او را نمی‌دیدی و من هم که اهل باشگاه‌رفتن و رقص و قمار نبودم فقط در همین کتاب‌خانه به‌اش برخورد می‌کردم که رفته‌رفته آشنا شدیم و به هم گرم گرفتیم و او سال‌ها بعد در تهران در خریدوفروش زمین زیاد موفق شد، و هم‌چنین شد نمایندهٔ مجلس.

گفتم «اون‌جا به انگلیسی کتاب گیر می‌آد.»

گفت «اما فیتز جرالد خوب درآورده.»

گفتم «اگر صدای شعر مهم باشه از لحاظ صدای شعر نمی‌دونم. خوبیش را نمی‌دونم، از لحاظ جفت‌گیری کلمه هم آن‌قدرها انگلیسی نمی‌دانم که بدانم چه‌قدر دقیق کلمه انتخاب کرده. ولی از لحاظ کلام، شعرها شعرهای اصلی نیست. شاید به حسب ذوق، شاید به اقتضای کلمه و آهنگ، شاید به علت ندانستن درست فارسی، او از بعضی معنی‌ها صورت‌های تازه ساخته، ترکیب تازه‌یی داده، یعنی درواقع شعر تازه‌یی گفته. من گمون می‌کنم که روحیه آن شعرها را که پیش خود فهمیده بوده یا

I said, "I imagine so. I don't know, probably. I have only read that he really liked them. So much so that he called a collection of his poems the *West-Eastern Divan*[11], or some such name."

"*Divan?*"

"It means a collection of poems, in one sense."

"That's interesting. Any of them in there?" So saying, he pointed to the end of the hall and the library I had earlier identified. It was a good, large and peaceful library, full of books, where you could read a book quietly and see no other readers. Its director was a calm and quiet Iranian, who would not be seen in other parts of the city, such as venues for playing sport or tennis or swimming, and since I too was no fan of clubs and dancing or gambling, I would only run across him in the library, and gradually we became acquainted and grew closer, and in later years, he became very prosperous by buying and selling land in Tehran, and he also became a member of parliament.

I said, "There you can find books in English."

He said, "But FitzGerald has done a good job."

"If the sound of the poem is important, I am not sure about his translation. Not sure how good it is, in terms of matching words—I don't know enough English to know how rigorously he has picked his words. But in terms of meaning, the poems are not the same as the original. Maybe because of personal preference or maybe because of words and the rhythm, maybe because he did not know Persian well enough, he has rendered some of the poems in a different form, creating new combinations, meaning that in essence he created new poems. I think the spirit of the poems as he understood them in his mind, or as he

---

11. In 1814, Goethe had his first experience with Persian poetry and became so awed by that tradition that he soon published his *West-Eastern Divan*, considered by many as one of his masterpieces. English translations of the book exist. See for example, Johann Wolfgang von Goethe, *West-Eastern Divan*, Tr. by Eric Ormsby, (New York, Gingko Publisher, 2019).

فرض می‌کرده، و تازه و بی‌سابقه بوده در زبان انگلیسیِ معمول شعر، وقتی به
انگلیسی درآورده گُل کرده. شاید از این بهتر هم نمی‌شده. ولی خیام چیز
دیگری‌ست.»

گفت «جالبه.»

گفتم «شاید چیزی که باعث شهرتش شده همان جوردیگربودن نگاه
و قطع شعر در این ترجمه است که در زبان انگلیسی مثلش را نداشتند، اگر
نداشتند، آن‌جوری، تا آن‌وقت. شاید. اگر درست می‌گویم. درهرحال ما
در زبانمان عادت داریم در شعر به یک‌جور آهنگ و وزن که من در شعرهای
شما، نه شما خودتان، مقصودم نه شخصاً شما، در شعرهای زبان‌هایی که
کمی به‌شان آشنا هستم، انگلیسی تاحدی، پیدا نمی‌کنم. شاید هم این
عیبِ درست‌زبان‌ندانستنم باشد. سخته زبان را درست‌دانستن، حتی زبان
مادری‌مان را درست‌دانستن. درهرحال هر زبانی امکان‌هایی داره که در
زبان‌های دیگر نیست، عیناً.»

گفت «جالبه. چه‌طور؟»

می‌خواستم داد بزنم که مُردم و مُردی ازبس که جالبه گفتی. اما
گفتم «چه‌طور می‌شه

"Les sanglots longs des violons de l'automne" را به انگلیسی
یا به آلمانی یا روسی یا ایتالیائی گفت، با همین آهنگ و با همین اثر که از
آهنگ می‌گیریم؟ چه‌جور می‌شود گفت

Stars! hide your fires

let not light see my deep and black desires

به فرانسه یا فارسی یا هر زبان دیگری که این‌جور کلمه‌ها با همین معنی
همه تک‌هجائی باشند و بیایند و هرکدام معنی مشخص خودشان را مثل میخ
بنشانند در مغز گیرنده؟»

thought he understood them, were so fresh and unprecedented in the common language of English poetry that his translation has been so popular. Maybe it was impossible to do any better. But Khayyam is something else."

He said, "That's interesting."

I said, "Maybe what made the translation famous was the uniqueness of its vision and form of presentation since nothing like it had existed in the English language, till then; if, of course, I am right and in fact it hadn't existed in the English language. Anyway, in the poetry in our language, we are used to a certain music and rhythm that I find lacking in your poems, and I don't mean you personally, but in the poetry of the languages I am a bit familiar with, like English. Maybe the problem is that I don't know the languages well enough. It is hard to know a language well; even to know one's mother tongue well. Anyway, every language has certain possibilities that do not necessarily exist in another language. Or not exactly."

He said, "That's interesting. How 'not exactly'?"

I wanted to cry out and say you're killing me, and killing yourself with this incessant use of "interesting." But instead, I said, "How can you say, 'Les sanglots longs / Des violons / De l'automne'[12] in English, or German, or Russian, or Italian? With the same music and the same effect we take from it. How can you say, 'Stars, hide your fires / Let not light see my deep and black desires'[13] in French or Persian or any other language so that the words are all, like the original, monosyllabic and each can nail the meaning in the mind of the listener?"

---

12. From "Chanson d'automne" (Autumn Song), 1866, by Paul Verlaine. While the poem was already famous in France, after the end of the Second World War, it became legendary. It was revealed that these lines, as well as the lines after it (*"Blessent mon Coeur / D'une langueur / Monotone."*), were used as a coded radio message to the French Resistance signaling that D-Day, the Allied invasion of Normandy, is twenty four hours away.

13. William Shakespeare, *Macbeth*, Act I, Scene 4, lines 333–4.

مدتی ساکت ماند. توی لیوانش نگاه می‌کرد و بعد سر کشید و لیوان خالی در دستش را نگاه می‌کرد. دست تکان دادم که پیش‌خدمت بیاید و وقتی رسید سفارش دوتا دیگر به‌هاش دادم که رفت و آمد و آورد و رفت و ما سکوتمان را به لب‌زدن به لیوان‌هایمان فرو شستیم.

گفت «شاعر وقتی شعر گفته به قصد این‌که کسی ترجمه‌ش کنه که نگفته. از داخل خودش گفته، از داخل خودش می‌گه.»

گفتم «حتی برای خودش تنها.»

گفت «حتی برای خودش تنها. اگر که شاعره.»

گفتم «اگر که شاعره.» و بعد گفتم «ترجمه یه چیز تازه‌س. با اختراع چاپ و افزایش وسیله‌های پخشه که مطرح شده، زیاد. نقاشی را نمی‌شه تغییر شکل داد به صورتی که رواج داره در یك جای دیگه‌یی. همین‌طور آواز و موسیقی. البته.» حرف ما از هرکجا که می‌گفتیم یواش‌یواش کشیده شد به این که بر سر یك شعر از ترجمه چه‌ها می‌آورند، در ترجمه چه استحاله‌یی پیدا می‌کند یك شعر.

پرسید «شما خودتان شعر می‌گین؟»

گفتم «نه.»

پرسید «نقاشی؟»

گفتم «نه.»

پرسید «موسیقی؟»

گفتم «یکی از تصمیم‌های درستی که در زندگی گرفته‌ام همین نخواندنِ درس موسیقی‌نواختن بود.»

گفت «ها!؟»

گفتم «آره. پدرم برام یه ویولون خرید و معلم گرفت که یاد بگیرم. سه روز رفتم. ازبس زیاد پیشرفت کردم زیاد ترسیدم.»

«ترس؟»

For a while he remained silent. He gazed into his glass and drank it down, then looked at the empty glass in his hand. I waved my hand to summon the waiter, and when he arrived, I ordered two more drinks, and he left, came back [with our order], and departed, and we both washed away our silence by sipping at our new glasses.

He said, "When a poet writes a poem, he doesn't write it so that someone can translate it. He writes it from inside himself. He writes it from inside himself."

"Even for himself alone." I said

He said, "Even for himself alone. If he is really a poet."

I said "If he is a real poet." Then I said, "Translation is a new thing. It is with the invention of the printing press and the increase in means of reproduction that it has become popular, very popular deal. You can't change the form of a painting to a form more prevalent somewhere else. The same for songs and music, of course." Our conversation, regardless of where we began, eventually came back to what happens to a poem when it is translated, what process of transfiguration it undergoes.

"Do you yourself write poetry?"

"No," I said.

"Paint?" He asked.

"No," I said

"Play music?" He asked.

I said, "One of the best decisions I ever made was to not have any music lessons."

"Ha?" He said.

I said, "Yes. My father bought me a violin and he hired a teacher so that I could learn. I attended for three days. I improved so much that I became very frightened."

"Frightened?"

«ترس. چون دیدم باید زیاد جدی بود، و جدی‌بودن برای خوب‌ویولون‌زدن لابد مرا از ورزش و پرسه با دوچرخه و از بعضی دنبال‌کردن‌های دیگه محروم می‌کنه. نخواستیم. درعوض گفتیم بشنویم، و درست بشنویم بهتره تا بد و خراب بنوازیم.»

«جالبه.»

عاجز شدم، گفتم «خیلی. واقعاً خیلی. چه‌چیز بدتر از بدصدادرآوردن؟»

خندید. آبجو بود که نرمش کرد؟ پرسید «پس چه می‌کنید؟»

پرسیدم «کی؟ کجا؟ در چه موردی؟» اما نپرسیدم برای چه می‌پرسد. فکر کردم شاید حس کند که می‌خواهم از من سئوال خصوصی نداشته باشد، و این ناراحتش کند که من فکر کرده باشم که او دارد. این بود که قصدم از این سئوالم، کمی، سربه‌سر گذاشتن بود. آبجو و شکم خالی‌ام اثر گذاشته بود روی گردش خونم و من، کمی، در اختیار سرخوشی اولش بودم. اما برای این‌که چنین حس در باره‌ام نداشته باشد گفتم «کتاب می‌خوانم، تنیس می‌زنم، شنا می‌کنم. دنیا را نگاه می‌کنم. دریایی زیر پنجره‌ام نیست که تُف در آن بیاندازم.»

به‌سرعت فهمید که دارم به یک گفته از خودش اشاره می‌کنم. چشمان براقش تند نگاه جرقه‌دار به من کردند اما نه از سر آزردگی، یا غیظ. حتی شاید می‌شد انگار نوعی سپاس، یا دست کم قبول، در آن‌ها دید. گفتم «در دو جبهه عشق می‌ورزیم و امیدواریم که این فن شریف چون هنرهای دگر مایهٔ حرمان نشود.» از این فن شریف به بعد، که خود بی‌اختیارِ من آمد، به اصل فارسی‌اش آمد، و پیش از آن‌که چیز دیگری گفته باشم چشمان جرقه‌اندازش مرا وارسی می‌کرد، انگار می‌پرسید یعنی چه؟ برایش دست‌وپاشکسته ترجمه کردم.

پرسید «از همان حافظ؟»

گفتم «از همان حافظ.» و از درک تند و مستقیم‌اش خوشم آمد. گفتم «ما اصلاً بهش فال می‌گیریم. سئوال می‌کنیم ازش برای آینده. خنده‌داره، نه؟ با او مشورت می‌کنیم در هرکار. عادت کرده‌ایم. مثل لهجه‌های محلی شده است این عادت. مهم هم نیست که این کار عاقلانه نباشد. سرگرمی خوبی که

"Frightened. Because I realized you have to be very serious and being serious about playing the violin, well, it would probably deprive me of the time to spend on sports and cycling around and other pursuits. We didn't want it. Instead we said we'd prefer to listen and thought it was better to listen well than to play badly, dissonantly."

"That's interesting."

Growing frustrated, I said, "Much better. So much better. What is worse than making dissonant sounds."

He laughed. Had the beer softened him? He asked, "Then what do you do?"

I asked, "When, where, in what capacity?" But I did not ask why he was asking. I thought he might think I did not want him to ask me questions about private matters, and that he might feel hurt again, thinking that I thought he was prying. My real intention in asking the question was to tease him a little. The beer on an empty stomach had gone to my head and I was now tipsy from its initial buzz. To make sure he harbored no hard feelings about me, I said, "I read books, play tennis, swim, watch the world. There is no sea under my window to spit in."

He soon realized I was quoting some of his own words. His bright eyes flashed a fast, piercing glance at me, but not in dismay, or anger. Even maybe a hint of gratitude or acceptance could be detected in them. I said, "We love on two different fronts and hope that this noble trade won't, like other trades, cause sorrow and grief." From "this noble trade" onwards, the poem flowed without my control, and it came out in its original Persian, and before I could say anything else, he was, again, looking me over, with those flashing eyes, as if he was asking, what does it mean! I offered a tangled translation.

"From that same Hafez?" he asked.

"From that same Hafez," I said, and I liked his quick, clear, and sharp comprehension. I said, "We even tell our fortunes with his poetry. We ask it questions about our future. It's funny, no? We consult it on every matter. It has become a custom. We

هست. فرصت می‌شود که شعر بخوانیم. حالا اگر شعر را درست نفهمیم، آن حرف دیگری است.»

پرسید «کتابش به زبانش در آن کتاب‌خانه هست بگیریم؟»

پرسیدم «به فارسی؟ به فارسی برای چه می‌خواهید؟»

گفت «برای این که بشنوم. برایم ازش بلند بخوانید، یک‌خرده. بشنوم چه‌جور طنین دارد.»

پرسیدم «فقط برای همین؟»

گفت «آره، برای همین. هم‌چنین برای همین.»

گفتم «کتابش این‌جا نیست. از حفظ می‌خوانم.»

گفت «چه‌جور انتخاب می‌کنید؟»

گفتم «خودش می‌آد. یه سی ـ چهل‌تائی هسن اون‌جا تو یاد، میان خودشون. هرکدوم اومد. تا اون‌جا که به یادم بیاد.» و شروع کردم به «مژدۀ وصل تو...» را خواندن. و تا آخرش خواندم. چرا این؟ چون روی سنگ گورش است و سال‌ها سال و هر باری که سر کتاب باز می‌کردی به فال‌گرفتن، نقر روی سنگ قبرش را و کتیبه‌های دورتادور حیاط مقبره‌اش را برای جمع‌کردن توجه و تمرکز حواس به یاد می‌کشاندی، به‌شان خیره می‌ماندی انگار اقامه و قنوت این نماز جانانه‌ات باشند اگر چه رعب وصف «کنج عزلت که طلسمات عجایب دارد» همیشه می‌لرزاندت و «از کران تا به کران لشکر ظلم است ولی از ازل تا به ابد فرصت درویشان است» تو را پیش منظر بی‌انتهای کل آفرینش و هستی مبهوت می‌گذاشت از این دید ترسناک واقع‌بین، و استواریت می‌داد از آن صبر سرمد و توکل بی‌تردید، و بعد شد که ظلام خرافه‌ها رفتند و خوبی‌ها را نگاه داشتیم و مثل

are used to it. It has become like a local dialect, this custom of ours. It doesn't matter if it isn't rational. It is at least good entertainment. It is an occasion for us to read poetry. Whether we understand the poem correctly is another matter entirely."

He asked, "Is his book, in his language, in the library for us to borrow?"

I said, "In Persian? What do you want to do with the Persian?"

He said, "So that I can hear it. Read me aloud from it, a little. To hear how it sounds."

"Just for this?"

"Yes, just for this. But also for this."

"His book isn't here. I'll recite from memory."

"How will you know what to pick?"

"It comes of its own accord. I have some thirty, forty of his poems stored in my memory. They come by themselves, in no particular order. As much as I can remember." And I begin reciting "The tidings of consummation with you."[14] And I recited it all the way to the end. Why this one? Because it is on his gravestone, and for years, every time you opened the book to ask your fortune, you remembered the inscription chiseled on the gravestone and the writings on the walls around his grave, all intended to focus your thoughts and attention, and you gazed at them as if they were the embodiment of your heartfelt prayer though that line "The corner of solitude has magical powers" brought fear and trembling to your heart, along with the line "from one end to another, all armies of injustice," while "from eternity to eternity is the hour of the Darvish[15]" brought you

14. For the complete poem in English and Persian, see *Faces of Love: Hafez and the Poets of Shiraz*, bilingual edition, trans. Dick Davis (Washington, D.C.: Mage Publishers, 2019), pp. 234–5.

15. While in today's vernacular, the word "*darvish*" often conjures the kitsch phenomenon of the "Whirling Dervishes," in the context

جان ارزش گذاشتیم که جان ارزشش به درک آنها بود. و اکنون در این برهوت فلز داغ و بوی دود و تبهکاریِ کشیدن رمق آدمیت از آدم به ضرب آز و جبر گردش گردونهٔ مصنوعِ آدمی که خداوندگار آدمی شده است و بندِ زندگیِ در اسارتِ انسانِ درمانده را به خود بسته است پناه و رفاه می‌جستم از زیبائی و صفا و ذروه علو حس و فکرهایی که طور و قدس و کوثر و ملکوت و فرشتگان تصویرهای عامی آنها بود. تا آخر تمام را خواندم اما هر مصراع را که می‌خواندم حس می‌کردم برای خودم بار اولی است، انگار، که برخورد می‌کنم با آن، مثل همیشه در هربار اما از این درک نافذ گیرنده که هربار در تکرار تازه و نویافته می‌آید صدایم شکسته می‌شد و در جانم تقلا بود که شرم از چشم‌هام نریزد. تا آخر که خواندم گفتم «این روی سنگ قبرش است.»

پرسید «کی مرد؟»

گفتم «کی گفته او مرده؟»

هیچ نگفت.

گفتم «حدس می‌زنم که فکر می‌کنید احساساتی‌ام، یا شده‌ام. ولی فکر نمی‌کنم باشم.»

face to face with the entirety of creation and existence and you stood in awe of this frighteningly realistic vision, and then it consoled you with its heavenly patient and unshakable faith, and it was then that the darkness of superstition lifted and we saw what was good in those writings and valued them as dear life, since the key to life was in understanding them. And now in this wasteland of hot metal and the stench of smoke and the perfidy of depriving humans of their humanity by force of greed, and the deterministic movement of the man-made machinery that has now become the new divinity over them, and has tied to itself the chains of desperate enslaved humanity, and in that divinity we seek solace and comfort, but everything from beauty and sincerity and sublime sensations and the thoughts that begot Tur and Qods and Kosar,[16] and heaven and angels were all widespread manifestations of the same common human imagination. I recited the poem to the end, but every line I recited was, for me, as if I was encountering it for the first time, and like each and every other time that I had encountered it, this sharp perceptive vision seemed still fresh and newly discovered, and my voice broke and, in my soul, there was a struggle lest my shame poured from my eyes. When I reached the end, I said, "This is written on his gravestone."

"When did he die?"

"Who said he is dead?"

He said nothing.

I said, "I guess you think I am or have become emotional. But I don't think I have."

---

of the Persian classical poetry, used here, it implies impervious disregard for all worldly attachments.

16. These are Qur'anic/Biblical references. Tur is Mount Sinai, where Moses is thought to have received the Ten Commandments. Qods is both a term for Heaven and the Arabic name for Jerusalem. Kosar is a river in Heaven from which spring waters are said to flow.

گفت «می‌شه چیزهایی‌ش را برام ترجمه کنین؟» از روی حرف آخرم پریده بود.

پراکنده ترجمه کردم، بی‌ربط سطر پشت سطر، بد. البته بد. «به ولای تو» یا «ابر هدایت» یا لطافت تصور و تصویر و ذره‌نمائی از نهایت عظمت که در «پیش‌تر زان‌که چو گردی ز میان برخیزم» است را چه‌گونه می‌شد به انگلیسی یا به هر شکل در هر زبان و ازجمله در همین فارسی گفت که قصابیِ کلام نباشد؟ گفتم «در این قالب که غزل اسمش است ربط ظاهری میان سطرها مطرح نیست. پهلویِ‌هم‌آوردن دسته‌یی فکر و مایه در یک حس. نوعی سیلان شعور. الان فقط یک غزل در یادم است که از ابتداش تا آخر آشکار به هم بسته‌اند.» و بی‌آن‌که خواسته باشد خواندم «یاری اندر کس نمی‌بینیم...» تا آخر.

گفت «درهرحال موسیقی کلام مطلقاً گیراست.»

بی کلمه‌یی به‌گفتن‌آوردن، از ذهن می‌گذشت که افسوس در توانائی زبانیِ تو نیست که دریابی ـ و با تمام حجم و هیأت هرسورونده و دوّار و درعین‌حال ثابت از صلابت و سیالی و صیقلی‌اش، که بازتابندهٔ تصویر هستی و بینای خیره به دیدار چه بسیار گوشهٔ مشهود و ناپیداست دریابی ـ یا دست کم به پیش بیایی و بخوانی و مسخر و مسحور بمانی از این «آب حیوان تیره‌گون شد خضر فرخ‌پی کجاست» از «لعلی از کان مروت برنیامد، سال‌هاست»، از «صدهزاران گل شکفت و بانگ مرغی برنخاست»، از «کس به میدان درنیامد، سواران را چه شد؟» که شنیدم گفت:

He said, "Can you translate some of it for me?" He had ignored my last comment.

I translated, haphazardly, line by line, badly, of course badly. How can such constructs as "Swear to your grace?" or the "cloud of guidance," or the softness of image and vision and the ability to capture in one fragment the entire majesty of existence, like the line "Before I disappear like a speck of dust," be translated into English or any other language, including rendering it in Persian, without butchering the words. I said, "In this form that is known as a ghazal there is no apparent connection between each line. It is a way of bringing together a collection of thoughts and ideas in one expressive poem. It is a kind of stream of consciousness. At this precise moment, I can recall only one ghazal in which, from the beginning to the end, the thoughts and ideas are closely related." And without being asked, I recited "I see no love in anyone" in its entirety.[17]

He said, "Anyway the music of the words is absolutely enthralling."

Without saying a word about it to him, it occurred to me it was a shame he did not have the language to understand the poetry in Persian—and understand it in the full might and majesty of its ever-questioning and overarching insight that was at once constant in its sharpness, salience, and sparkling perception, but also reflective of the entirety of existence as it fastened its wondrous gaze upon the manifest and hidden corners of the world, and he couldn't even come forth and recite and be humbled and mesmerized by "Life's water's muddied now, and where / Is Khezr[18] to guide us from despair?" or "For years no rubies have been found / In stony mines deep underground" and "No rider comes to strike it; where / Is everyone who should be there?" When I heard him say:

---

17. For the complete poem in English and Persian, see *Faces of Love*, trans. Davis, pp. 10–13.

18. Khezr is a figure in the Qur'an who is a contemporary of Moses. His name means "the green man."

«حسش را از حسی که می‌کنید گرفتم.»

چیزی نگفته بودم من. آیا این را از او شنیده بودم من؟ نمی‌دانم. نپرسیدم. سکوت نشان داده بود که گویاست، بهتر که قدرتش را نگه دارد.

یك چند لحظه بعد گفت «نمی‌خورید؟»

لیوان دومم هنوز لب‌نخورده روی میز بود. گفتم «گفتید موسیقی کلام در آن شعرها گیراست. موسیقی کلام گاهی گمراه‌کننده ست، تاحدی.»

«چه؟»

«عادت می‌کنیم به موسیقی‌ش، و از معنی‌ش دور می‌مانیم موسیقی‌ش جا می‌دهد ازیك‌سو به نقاشی از چشم‌انداز، که این مثل نقش قالی و کاشی برایمان خودش زیباست، ازسوی‌دیگر در تنگنا می‌اندازد بیان را — اگر بیان اصلاً به‌دردبخور باشد. چون شعر ما به شمار هجا زیاد کار ندارد. این ربط آهنگی کلمه است و ترتیبش که می‌سازد. حالا باید این با فکر و حس عجین شود تا شعر بسازد. شبه‌شعر پیش ما خداخوردار. اما میان این شبه‌شعرها هم تصور و تصویرهای با قدرت فراوان به دست می‌آید. عشق، آدمی‌گری، غم، غیظ، شادی، همه فراوان است. میدان و وسعت میدان زندگی از آن سوی جیحون بگیر تا انتهای آناتولی، برو تا زیر رشته‌قفقاز، بیا تا خلیج فارس، برو تا هند برای فارسی‌زبان و سرایندهٔ نظم و شعر به فارسی سراینده بوده است و قرن‌هاقرن، بیش از هزار سال دوام آورده است. درنتیجه محصولش حتی کشمنی، کیلوئی، زیاد. خیلی زیاد. گاهی بی‌جهت زیاد. جالب؟ کمابیش همیشه جالب، بسیاروقت‌ها هم‌چنین ارزش‌دار. گاهی در یك قطعهٔ صدسطری که نه خیلی زیاد گیرنده است می‌رسی به یك پرواز، به یك تکه سنگ که یاقوت است یا الماس. هزار سال پیش از این امروز گفت:

"I felt the feeling from the feeling you expressed."

I had said nothing. Had I heard him speak? I don't know. Did not ask. Silence had shown its eloquence—better now to honor it.

A few moments later he said, "You don't want to drink?"

My second glass, still untouched, was on the table. "You said the music of words in these poems is enthralling. But the music of words is at times a bit misleading," I said.

"What do you mean?"

"We become accustomed to its music, and stray from its meaning, and the music leads to a kind of painting of a landscape, which in itself, like the design of a [Persian] carpet or tiles, is beautiful, yet at the same time it limits the articulation of the words, if indeed there is any use for articulation here. Because in our poetry we don't worry much about the number of syllables. The rhythmic structure and order of the words are what create the music. With this must also come ideas and sensations to then make a poem. Pseudo-poetry in our tradition is a dime a dozen. But even in these pseudo-poems powerful images and ideas can be found. Love, humanism, melancholy, anger, joy, are also in abundance. In terms of the area it covers, on one side the poetry goes from Jeyhoun to the end of Anatolia, all the way to the borders of the Caucasus, while on the other side it stretches from the Persian Gulf all the way to India, and above all, there have been Persian-speaking poets and versifiers who have for century upon century continued to create poetry, so that it has survived for more than a thousand years. As a result, what has been produced, if one were to measure it by weight and in kilos, has been a great deal. Very much indeed. At times uselessly much. Is it always interesting? Almost always. And often valuable too. Sometimes in a poem of a hundred lines that doesn't have much else to recommend it you come across a soaring couplet, a pebble that turns out to be a ruby, or even a diamond. A thousand years ago, one poet said:

بسان کوه بپای و بسان لاله بخند

بسان چرخ بتاز و بسان ابر ببار

صد سال و بیش‌تر و پیش‌تر از او هم دیگری می‌گفت:

بی صدهزار مردم تنهائی

با صدهزار مردم تنهائی

تفاوت روحیه. دستور زندگانی محکم، درست. حس‌های آدم تنها، همیشه منفرد میان مردم ـ بقیه مردم. بگیریم آن یاقوت، این الماس، خیلی هم تراشیده.»

گفت «فوق‌العاده.»

گفتم «نه در این ترجمۀ تندِ سرپائی، جادرجا.» و بعد گفتم «اگر این‌ها را به عادی‌ترین زبان امروزی‌مان درست می‌آد به یه دسته کلمه‌های دیگه‌ای از همین زبان دربیارم از این صفا و سادگی نظم و این بیان درخشنده، که در اصل فارسی‌شان بسیار درخشنده‌س می‌افتن.»

گفت «کلمه‌س ابزار کار ما، به‌هرصورت. فوق‌العاده بود، به‌هرصورت.»

خواستم بگویم چه خوب کردی که آن «جالبه»هایت را به این «فوق‌العاده» گفتنت عوض کردی. اما نگفتم و گفتم «ولی خُب به حسب اقتضای روز و حس و حال شخصی شاعر کار بیش‌تر منحصر شد به جفت‌گیری ضرب و صدای کلمه‌ها، که گاهی به حد قدرتی بی‌نظیر، بی‌نظیر بی‌نظیر، رسیده.»

«ابستراکسیون؟»

«تاحدی،»

«موسیقی؟»

درست نفهمیدم، پرسیدم «یعنی؟»

گفت «یعنی صدای انسان به جای ساز.»

Like a mountain endure, and like a lilac laugh,
Like a wheel whirl, and like a cloud drizzle.

A hundred years, or even more, before him, someone
    else said,

Without a hundred thousand people, solitude;
With a hundred thousand people, solitude.

The difference in spirit between one person and another. A commandment for life, solid and accurate too, encapsulating the feelings of the lonely individual, always alone among people— other people. Behold that ruby, this diamond, and so beautifully cut.

He said, "Remarkable."

I said, "Not in this quick, haphazard, disorderly translation."

And then I said, "If I try to turn these lines that fit perfectly in our everyday language today into another set of words in the same language, the grace and simplicity of the structure, the shimmering articulation that shines in the original Persian is lost."

He said, "Words are in any case the stuff of our work. It was remarkable, anyway."

I wanted to say how kind of him to change his "interesting" to this "remarkable." But I didn't and instead only said, "Well, according to the [literary] conventions of the times, and the personal mood and feelings of the poet, the work was solely about matching the beat with the sound of the words, sometimes to a level of matchless competence, matchless, matchless, matchless."

"Abstraction?"

"To a degree."

"Music?"

I didn't quite understand. I asked, "Meaning?"

He said, "Meaning the human voice in lieu of a musical instrument."

«آواز؟»

«یعنی تلفظ کلمه به جای نغمه و آهنگ.»

گفتم «نه تا آن حد. ولی گاهی نزدیك به آن حد. تا آن حد که کلمه‌ها و جفت‌گیری‌شان گذشته از حالت، معنا هم دارن ـ هرچند بیش‌تر وقت‌ها پرت. با حس‌های کمابیش ابتدائیِ ساده که این طبیعیه که پرت باشن، هم. بیش‌تر.»

گفت «مقصود من یك ابستراکسیون جدی‌تره. رفتن کلمه به جایی که، درمَثَل، باخ رفته در ساخت موسیقی.»

گفتم «من از باخ چیزی نشنیده‌ام.»

تکان تندی خورد. با تعجب پرسید «نه؟»

گفتم «نه. به جز یك تکه.»

گفت «هزاروسیصد تکه کار داره.» انگار تأکید سرزنش‌دهنده روی ندانستنم می‌کرد.

گفتم «آن‌قدر؟ چرا آن‌قدر؟»

گفت «بعضی‌هاش سه ـ چهار ساعت هم دراز.» زنگِ سرزنش در صدایش بود. باز با تعجب پرسید «نه؟»

گفتم «نه. به جز یکی‌ش. صفحه‌ش را دارم، سه ـ چهار دقیقه می‌شه، ستوکفسکی در فیلم "فانتزیا".» و بعد گفتم «خیلی چیزاس که خیلی‌ها نشنیده‌ن، اصلاً نه.»

گفت «آره.» انگار از سرِ گذشت بود که تصدیقِ حرف من می‌کرد، شاید فهمیده بود اشاره‌ام به چه بسیار نشنیده‌های خودش بوده است.

گفتم «درهرحال موسیقی اساساً ابستراکسیون هس، خودش.»

سری جنباند که «شاید» یا «باشد»، ولی انگار حواسش جای دیگر بود.

"Song?"

"I mean enunciation of words rather than melody and songs."

I said, "No, not to that degree. But at times close to it. To the extent that occasionally the pairing of words, aside from conveying the mood, also carry meaning, although most of the time they don't make much sense. It is natural that the sense in lines expressing primitive simple feelings would be off, too, or more so."

He said, "I meant a more serious form of abstraction. Words entering a realm that Bach, for example, has entered in composing music."

I said, "I haven't heard anything by Bach."

With a sharp jolt of surprise, he asked , "Nothing?"

"Nothing, except one piece."

He said, "He has composed one thousand three hundred pieces." As if he was emphatically chiding me for my ignorance.

"That many? Why so many?" I said.

He said, "Some of the pieces are three to four hours long." An air of condescension was palpable in his voice. And with surprise he again asked, "Nothing?"

I said, "Nothing, save one piece. I have a recording of it. It is about three to four minutes long. Stokowski in the movie *Fantasia*." And then I said, "There are many things many people have never heard of, absolutely not heard of."

He said, "Yes." It was maybe out of pity that he was agreeing with me. Or maybe he had understood that my reference was to the many things he himself hadn't heard of.

I said, "Anyway, music is itself a form of abstraction, in itself."

He shook his head, as if to say, "Maybe" or "Agreed," but clearly his mind was elsewhere.

گفتم «در آوازخواندن ما میون شعرها، کلمه‌ها "دل ای‌دل" و "جانم جانم" می‌گیم، صدا غلت می‌دیم.» و دل ای‌دل و جانم را برایش ترجمه کردم گفتم «این ابستراکسیونه، خودش، تکرار. مقصودتون این بود، یعنی؟»

سری جنباند که «شاید» یا «ممکن است». شاید هم که «پُر می‌گی.» یا «پرت می‌گی.»

گفتم «نزدیك می‌شه به ابسترکسیون، ولی نه درست آن‌جوری که شما گفتین. شاید با کلمه درنمی‌آد، شاید. اصلاً شاید نشه.»

گفت «سعی کردن بشه. یا توی نقاشی.»

گفتم «شعرهای نزدیك به ابسترکسیون پیش ما نقاشی‌ان خودشون، نوعی. حتی وقتی وصفْ وصفِ واقعیته، ازقصد، چشم‌اندازِ کلیِ کار ابستراکسیون شده. با کلمه نقاشی. ولی ترتیب کلمه‌ها شرطه. تَرتیبه، اصلِ کار. یك نظمه اصلِ کار که خودش ابستراکسیون شده. بهش هم نظمَ می‌گیم، حتی. ولی می‌شه به اینا گفت شعر؟» سئوال نمی‌کردم، قبول نمی‌کردم که به آن‌ها بگویی شعر.

گفت «بستگی داره. چرا نشه؟ می‌گن می‌شه، همیشه نه، ولی می‌شه. نه کاملاً. تاحدي.»

گفتم «به‌هرحال ابستراکسیون، یك نوعیش، تو نقاشی‌های ما بوده. تو نقاشی‌های ما از قدیم هیچ‌وقت کوششی نبوده به آوردن شباهت کامل میان نقش و آن چیزی که ازش نقش می‌کردن. نمی‌بینی. نهی مذهبی هم بعدها بوده.»

گفت «نهی مذهبی ضدنقاشی تو تورات هم هس.»

گفتم «بعضی چیزهای مذهبی‌مون زیاد شباهت داره به همان تورات.»

گفت «می‌گن همه‌ش از خدا می‌آد.»

گفتم «می‌گن همه‌ش از خدا می‌آد.»

I said, "In our singing, we sometimes use phrases like *del ay del* or *janam, janam*, as we make the voice tremble."[19] And then I translated *del ay del* (heart, O heart) and *janam, janam* (love, O love') for him and said, "This is itself a form of abstraction and recreation. Is that what you meant?"

Shaking his head, he seemed to be saying, "Maybe," or "Possibly." Or maybe "You talk too much" or "You are off."

I said, "It comes close to abstraction, but not quite as you meant. Maybe it can't be realized in words, maybe it's just not possible."

He said, "They have tried to do so. Or as in painting."

I said, "Poems that are near abstraction in our tradition are themselves a painting, a kind of painting. Even when a poem is depicting reality, it appears overall as a form of abstraction. Painting with words. But the order of the words is the key. The order is the essence of the work. The verse is the essence of the work and it itself has become an abstraction. We even call it verse *nazm*. But can you even call this poetry?" I wasn't asking so much as refusing to accept that it could be called poetry.

He said, "It depends. Why can't it? They say it can be done— not always, but it can. Not completely, but to a certain extent."

I said, "Anyway, abstraction, one kind of abstraction, existed in our paintings. In our paintings, from the past, there was never any attempt to create a perfect likeness between the drawing and the subject. You never see it [in these paintings.]. The religious prohibition came only afterwards."

"The prohibition against painting is also in the Torah."

"Some of our religious things are similar to those in the Torah."

"They say it all comes from God," He said

I said, "They say it all comes from God."

---

19. *Tahrir* is a Persian singing technique similar to yodeling or tremolo.

دوباره نگاه تکان‌خورده‌یی به من انداخت. خندیدم. گفتم «از هرکجا. به هر علت. خداها تو مذهب‌ها یکی نیستن. مثل هم نیستن. یکی‌شون هفت ـ هشت‌تا دستداره، یکی‌شون پسر داره. یکی‌شون هم نه زاییده و نه زاییده شده و تنهاس.»

گفت «تنهابودن درست‌تره. دست‌هاش وازتره ـ هرچندتایی که داشته باشه.»

بعد، بعدتر بود که ملتفت شدم که چه گفته است. گفتم «سخت‌تره، ولی.» نگاهم کرد. لبخندی زد، سری جنباند، گفت «زیبائی زیادتری داره. زیبائی زیادتری می‌خواد، می‌سازه.»

«تنهابودن یا چنددست‌بودن؟»

خندید و گفت «شبیه‌درنیاوردن ولی درست‌درآوردن. زیبائی زیادتری می‌خواد.»

گفتم «توجیه می‌خواد. تو نقاشی‌های ما درخت و گل و گیاه، کوه، اسب، پرنده، ابر، اژدها، خیال، نه فقط آدم، خیال هم حتی ـ همه مشخصن با رنگ. رنگ‌هایی که مثل هرچه هس نیسّن. زبان کار شده این‌جور. تو نقاشی‌های ما هرچه هس بی‌شباهته به هرچه که هس. شبیه نیستن کاملاً، یعنی.»

گفت «به جهنم!» ناگهانی بود. خنده‌ام گرفت خوشم آمد. هیچ نگفتم.

گفت «ازنوساخته. چرا شبیه؟ چیزی که هس هس، دیگه. چرا تقلید؟ یك آفریدن تازه. یك آفریدن دوباره و ازنو. تجرد به ضرب جاروکردن زیادی‌ها. رسیدن به راستی، با دو بُعد سه بُعد و بیش‌تر درآوردن. دیدن فردی و شخصی خیال و جسم. یك دید و درك و حس چکیده، شخصی، خصوصی، فردی»

گفتم «فردی‌بودن عیبش این شده که جدا شده از واقع.»

گفت «شده که شده. شبیه پَخته. چرا شبیه؟»

Again, he gave me a look of surprise. I laughed and said, "Wherever and for whatever reason, God is not the same in different religions. Not alike. One has seven or eight hands, another has a son, and the other is neither begotten nor begot anyone, and is alone."

He said, "Being alone is more as it should be. His hands are freer—no matter how many He has."

Later, much later, I realized what he had said. I said, "It is more difficult, though."

He looked at me, smiled, moved his head and said, "It has more beauty, it requires more beauty, and creates more."

"Being alone or being multi-handed?"

He laughed and said, "Not creating an imitation but creating in the right way requires more beauty."

I said, "It requires elucidation. In our paintings trees, flowers, grass, mountains, horses, birds, clouds, dragons, every image, not just humans but even imagination [as rendered in painting], all are distinguished by their colors. Colors that are not like anything that exists in nature—a language has been developed this way. Whatever exists in our paintings is unlike anything that exists in reality; they are not an imitation, or not completely, that is."

"To hell with it." It was sudden; it made me laugh. I liked it, but I said nothing.

"It is recreating. Why imitate. What exists exists, after all. Why imitate? A new creation. A new creation and from the beginning. Abstraction by sweeping away all that is superfluous. Arriving at the truth, in two dimensions, or three dimensions, and then inventing even more. An individual personal vision of imagination and substance, a pure vision, cognition and sense, intimate, personal, and private."

I said, "The problem of individualizing is that it becomes estranged from reality."

He said, "So what? Imitation is flat. Why imitate?"

گفتم «شبیه را اگر ول کنیم جدا شده‌ایم از واقع.»

گفت «خودش می‌شه واقع. هیچ‌چیز جدا نمی‌شه از واقع. هرچه فکر کنیم، هرجور فکر کنیم از واقع میان، همه. جزء واقع‌اند همه.»

گفتم «هم جداشده از واقع هم، بدتر، عمومی‌شده در تمام کارهامون، فکرهامون. شده الگو. الگو شده، حتی. برای هرکاری، نه فقط شعر و نقاشی، هنر. بدجوری این ابستراکسیون، مطلق‌گوئی شده الگو. بی آن‌که خواسته باشیم اول، بی آن‌که ملتفت باشیم، اول. یا همین حالا، حتی. برای هر کاری. برای هر فکری.»

گفت «هرچه فکر کنیم، هرجور فکر کنیم، همه، از واقع میان. جزء واقع هسن، همه. حتی رؤیا.»

و گفتم «گمون نکنم این توضیح و شناختِ واقع باشه. برداشت هس. تصوره. گاهی. هم فقط همین، فقط. فقط همین، گاهی»

گفت «با همین تصور و برداشت‌هاس که جنبه‌های تازه‌ئی از واقعیت‌های نشناخته را می‌شناس، پیدا می‌کنن. چیزهایی که هس و ما اول نمی‌بینیم، نمی‌شناسیم ولی هسن.»

گفتم «این هم، خودش، همین، یعنی ابستراکسیون. یعنی بغرنج را ساده وانمود کنی. یعنی به‌سادگی قبول بغرنجی. یک‌جور قبول بغرنجی. قبول؟ نشناخته؟ بازنکردنِ پیچیده‌س. بازنکردنِ پیچیدگی.»

گفت «یا شاید هم شرط اول برای واکردن. قدم اولی.»

گفتم «بازنکردن. چه بازنکردن؟ ما از یک خیال که از ترس و جهل ما و ترس و جهل اجداد ما شروع شده شروع می‌کنیم، توش می‌مونیم و روش می‌سازیم. خیال اولی را سبک‌سنگین نمی‌کنیم. قبول می‌کنیم. با این قبول که درواقع قبول هم نیست بلکه مثل زبان و لهجه است که رشد می‌کنه در

I said, "If you give up imitation, you become estranged from reality."

He said, "It becomes real in itself. Nothing is ever estranged from the real. Whatever we think, it all comes from the real, it is all part of the real—everything."

I said, "Also estranged from the real—even worse, this state of affairs has seeped into everything we do, all our thoughts. It has become the model, for everything, not just in poetry and painting and the arts; this abstraction, this talking in absolutes, has sadly become a model for everything. Without us initially wanting it, without us initially even noticing. Even now, it is in everything, in every idea."

He said, "Whatever we think, however we think, it all comes from the real. Is part of the real. All of it. Even dreams."

I said, "I don't believe this is a true depiction or understanding of the real. It is an interpretation. It is a belief. At times just that. Just that, at times."

He said, "It's with these interpretations and beliefs that one discovers new aspects of unknown realities; one finds them, discovers things that exist, and we initially don't see, we don't recognize them, but they exist nonetheless."

I said, "This, too, itself, implies an abstraction; it means pretending that the complex is simple, facilely accepting complexity. A kind of acceptance of complexity. Accepting? Accepting means not knowing, means not unraveling the complex, not unraveling complexity."

He said, "Or maybe it's the first condition for unraveling. The first step."

I said, "Not unraveling. Unraveling what? We begin with an imagination rooted in our fears and ignorance, and the fears and ignorance of our ancestors, and we get stuck in it and build on it. We don't critically analyze that inherited imagination. We just accept it. With this acceptance—which in reality is not even acceptance, but more like a language and dialect that

ما، جلو می‌رویم. سئوال نمی‌کنیم. اگر هم بکنیم از ریشه نمی‌کنیم، از نتیجه می‌کنیم. ریشه را مطلق می‌گیریم. گرفته‌ایم. دربست قبول می‌کنیم، بهش فکر نمی‌کنیم و جلو می‌رویم. با این ابستراکسیون جلو می‌رویم. در این ابستراکسیون جلو می‌رویم. در زمانه جلو می‌رویم باهش، با زمانه جلو می‌ریم درش. زمانه‌س که جلو می‌ره. ما فقط گیریم. اما فکر می‌کنیم داریم می‌رویم. می‌پریم بالا. وقتی بیرون را ول کنی بری توی خودت توی خودت چه داری؟ از کجا داری؟ درون خودت ناچار خیالاته، اسمش را می‌گذارن معنویات، نه؟ با کلمه‌های معنی‌دار بیش‌تر می‌شه مجرد و مطلق گفت، از مجرد و مطلق گفت. ساختن خیال و تجرد و ابستراکسیون بیش‌تر قابل انتقال می‌شه با کلمه. ابستراکسیون در شعر ما کشیده به بخشیدنِ یك قدرت بی‌حدّ، در خیال، به نیروهای نامعلوم، نیروهایی که از تصور خود ما هسن، ساختهٔ خیال خود ما. ندانسته از روی الگوهایی که موجود داریم، گاهی تصادفی گاهی با مقداری وقت و انتخاب ناموجودها را می‌سازیم. از ناموجودهایی که ساختهٔ خیال خود ما هسن ترکیب تازه‌یی، که ناچار باز هم ناموجود هسن درواقع واقعیت می‌سازیم و حس و حرص و تمنا و حاجت خودمون را و قانون‌هایی را که فکر می‌کنیم لازم داریم و باید پیروی کنیم تا مسلط‌تر زندگی کنیم توی دهن آن‌ها می‌گذاریم. برای ضدیت و دشمنی‌ها و نفرت‌های خودمون هم همین کار را می‌کنیم. کم‌کم کار می‌رسه به جایی که این‌ها را روبه‌روی هم می‌گذاریم و می‌گیم، یاالله، دربیافتین به هم تا ببینیم ما چه باید بکنیم. سبك سنگین کردن‌های پوشیدهٔ خودمون را وامی‌گذاریم به اون‌ها تا ببینیم ما چه باید بکنیم. با روبه‌رو قراردادن قدرت‌هایی که فهمیده و نفهمیده با خیال می‌سازیم، و البته بیش‌تر نفهمیده و تصورکننده، اون‌ها را ضدهم هم تصور می‌کنیم... حتی می‌رسیم و می‌رسونیمشون به یك جور عشق‌های گُرگرفتهٔ نامعلوم.»

just grows in us—we move on. We don't question it. Even if
we do, we don't do it radically. We question the consequences.
The roots we assume to be absolutes. Have assumed this. We
accept it totally. We don't think about it. We merely move on.
We move on with this abstraction. We move on in this abstraction. Gradually, we move on with it. With time we move along
it. It is in fact time that moves, and we are just stuck in it. But
we think we are moving. That we are spiraling upward. If you
forfeit the outside and only delve inside yourself, what do you
have? Where do you get it from? Inside you there is only this
imagination, but they call it spirituality, no? With high-sounding
words you can more easily speak in abstractions and absolutes,
speak of abstraction and the absolute. Imagination, individuation,
and abstraction can all become more easily communicated with
words. Abstraction in our poetry has resulted in attributing, in
our imagination, an infinite power to unknown forces, forces
that emanate from our own imagination, from constructs of our
own imagination. From the models available to us we construct,
at times by accident and occasionally with the passing of time
and through choice, the non-existent. From these non-existent
entities that are in reality the constructs of our own imagination
we create new composites that are, by necessity, still constructs
of our imagination, but we turn them into reality and attribute to
them our own sensations and greed, our desires and needs, and
put in their mouth laws we think we need for a more comfortable
life. For our animosities and acrimonies and hatreds, we do the
same. Little by little, we reach a point that when we pit these
[imaginary forces] against another, and we say, for God's sake,
fight one another and let us know what we must do. To these
forces we attribute our own secret calculations, and then allow
them to decide what we must do. By pitting these forces—which
we have wittingly or unwittingly, and more often unwittingly,
simply concocted in our imagination—against each another,
and in our imagination, we even assume them to be actually in
conflict, and bringing ourselves and bringing them to a sort of,
love in flames, indeterminate."

پرسید «یعنی چه؟»

گفتم «کجاش یعنی چه؟»

پرسید «این عشق گُرگرفته. عشق گُرگرفته، خودش. نه؟»

گفتم «معنی‌کردنش سخته. درواقع سخت ساخته شده موضوع این سئوال در خیال، در وهم.»

پرسید «یعنی چه‌جور؟»

گفتم «چه‌جور بگم؟ درواقع پیچ‌دادن به ندانسته‌ها به جای ازهم‌بازکردن دانسته‌ها، به جای بازکردن و بازترکردن دانسته‌ها. پیچاندن ندانسته‌ها، به حدهای ظریف و زیبای تازه‌یی از ندانستن. همون زیبائی که می‌گفتین.»

پرسید «یعنی چه‌جور؟»

گفتم «مثلاً رفتن به توتر، یا بگو جلوتر؛ یا بگو بالاتر، به سمت دیگر، به شاخه‌های خیالی پیچیده‌تر نه تجربی، پس درنتیجه همان بودن و ماندن در ابستراکسیون، گیرکردگی در ابستراکسیون، مطلق‌بازی، در خیال‌های گیرکننده در بن‌بست، گیرکردگی در بن‌بست.»

پرسید «چه‌جور، مثلاً؟»

گفتم آخه چه‌جور بگم؟ بدون سابقه، بی آشنابودن سخته، هم گفتنش هم گرفتنش.»

باز گفت «مثلاً.»

گفتم «مثلاً عشق شیطان به خدا.»

تکان تندی خورد. پرسید «ها؟»

گفتم «آره. همین. همین دیگه. ساخته که شیطون از عشق شیطون شد. که شیطون عاشق خداست، اصلاً از عشق خداس که شر برای بشر درست کرده. شر درست کرده که بنده‌های خدا، از فرشته تا آدم، همه، برن گم شن تا تنها باشه با خدا خودش. نزدیك‌تر، بی‌دردسر، همیشه با خدا. به خدا می‌گه فرمانت را قبول نکردم من ‌—»

حرفم را برید پرسید «چه فرمانی؟»

"Meaning what?"

"What part do you mean?"

"This 'love in flames.' Love itself in flames. No?"

"Explaining it is hard. In reality, the subject of this question has itself, with difficulty, been constructed in the imagination, in illusion."

"In what way?"

"How can I put it? In reality by further complicating the unknowns instead of unraveling the knowns, instead of further and further unraveling the knowns. Complicating the unknowns, in intricate and beautiful new levels of not knowing. The same beauty you were talking about."

"How do you mean?"

"For example, delving deeper, or say further, or higher, in a different direction, to more crammed branches of the imagination, more complicated not more empirical, and thus being and remaining in abstraction, being stuck in abstraction, playing with absolutes, in imagination stuck at a dead-end, being stuck at a dead-end."

"How, for example?"

"Well, how can I say it? With no context, and no prior knowledge, it is hard, both articulating and grasping it."

Again, he said, "For example?"

"For example, the love of Satan for God."

Shifting sharply, he asked, "Ha?"

"Yes. This. Exactly this. It is said that Satan became Satan out of love. That Satan is in love with God. In fact it is out of this love of God that he created evil for humans. He has created evil so that all of God's servants, from the angels to Adam, can all get lost so that he can remain alone with his God. Closer. With no hangers-on. Always with God. He says to God, 'Your commandment I do not accept.'"

Interrupting me, he asked, "What commandment?"

گفتم «فرمانی که بهش بعد از خلق آدم داد.»

پرسید «چه فرمانی؟»

گفتم «در عقیده‌های مذهبی‌مان، در متن‌های مذهبی‌مان خدا به شیطان گفت کرنش به آدم کن، شیطان گفت نه، نمی‌کنم. خدا اوقاتش تلخ شد از آسمون انداختش پایین.»

پرسید «خدا از این کارها کرد؟ یادم نیست من.»

گفتم «اون‌وقت‌ها هنوز نبودیم ما.»

ابرویی بالا پراند. سری جنباند. گفت «خُب بعدش. چه شد بعدش وقتی از آسمان افتاد؟»

گفتم «پاش شکست.»

گفت «نه، چه شد بعدش وقتی که گفت قبول نکردم حرف را؟»

گفتم «فرمانت را، فرمانت را قبول نکردم، گفت. گفت قبول نکردم تا به من غضب کنی تا رودرروی هم باشیم، ازاین‌به‌بعد. همیشه. تا من بیش‌تر باشم با تو، در تماس باشم با تو. پهلوت باشم بیش‌تر. بیش‌تر باشم پهلوت. بیش‌تر بمونم پهلوت.»

نگاه پرسش و شگفت که در چهره داشت مکررتر و منتظرتر شد.

گفتم «همین. ابستره یعنی این. این ابسترس، دیگه. با کلمه‌هایی که فقط صدا نیسن. صدای فقط نیسن، معنی دارن، ولی، خُب، آبسترهن. این‌که شیطان از پس خدا دربیاد بهش بگه که به من به آدمی که آفریدی کرنش نمی‌کنم چون از او قدیمی‌ترم. اول مرا آفریدی تو، خدا. او را از خاک ساختی مرا از آتش آفریدی تو. او هم آفریدی که توی چنگ من باشه. نارو نزن به من که از کلکت من خبر دارم، و الا چرا آفریدیش از همون اول، زندگیش به من بسته‌س. بی من چکاره‌ست او؟ نه فقط چکاره‌س او، بی هر دو مون خودت چکاره‌یی، خدا؟ دلت سر میره بی ما. گفتی بهش کرنش بش کنم، نکردم من، از غرورم نبود این، ها. از عشق بود این. عشقم به تو، خودت، خدا، حواست کجاست؟ نافرمانیم از عشق بود، هم‌چنین

"The commandment He gives Satan after creating Adam."

"What commandment?"

"According to our religious beliefs, in our religious texts, God told Satan to bow before Adam. Satan said, 'No. I won't do it.' So God got angry and threw him out of heaven."

"God did this kind of thing? I don't remember."

"In those days we weren't yet around."

Raising one eyebrow, he moved his head and said, "Well, what next? What happened after he fell from the sky?"

"He broke his leg."

"No, what happened after he said, 'I don't accept Your word?'"

"Your commandment. 'Your commandment I do not accept,' he said. He said, 'I do not accept it, so that You will show Your wrath and then we will be, henceforth, head to head. Forever. So that I can be with You more, be in contact with You, be near You more. Be near You more; stay with You more.'"

The probing and surprised look on his face grew all the greater in the urgency of its anticipation.

I said, "Exactly. Abstraction is this. This is abstraction. With words that are not mere sounds. Are not just sounds, they have meanings, but they are after all abstractions. That Satan can stand up to God and tell Him, 'I will not bow to the human you have created, I will not bow. I won't because I am older than him. First You, God, created me. Him You created from mud and me You created from fire. You created him so that he would be in my clutches. Don't try to trick me; I know Your game. Otherwise, why did You create him in the first place? His life is tied to me. Without me who the hell is he? Not just who the hell is he, without both of us, who the hell are You, God? Without us, You will be bored. You told me to bow to him; I did not, but this was not out of pride, you must know. It was from love, this. My love for You, Yourself, God—what were You thinking of?

عقلم. عقلم گفت نکن تا غضب کنه. تا با غضب من و تو روبه‌روی هم باشیم، در خیالِ هم باشیم. در ربط با هم باشیم. تو سینهٔ هر مؤمن و هر کافر، آگاه و ناآگاه پهلوی هم باشیم. همیشه. نه مثل فرشته‌های دیگه‌ت فقط یکی از کارمندان دبیرخانهٔ خدائیت باشم. تو آدم بگی بکن این‌جور من بهش بگم نکن این‌جور، اون‌جوری بکن که من خودم بت می‌گم، اون‌جور. نه این که اون بهت گفته. اون‌وقت این‌جوری با تو، آخدا، من همیشه سرشاخم. درواقع با تو در کشتی‌گرفتنم، دائم. دائم در غلتیدنم با تو.»

وقتی که ساکت شدم یک چند لحظه ماند، بعد خنده‌اش ترکید.

گفتم «آره. ما اینیم!»

گفت «شیطان نبود که افتاد، آدم بود که بالا رفت. نگو هبوط، بگو عروج.»

گفتم «با یک شعر.»

گفت «با شعر این‌جوری. شعر. از شعر این‌جوری.» و باز می‌خندید و گفت «نبوغ یعنی این!»

پرسیدم «کدام‌شون.»

شاید در خنده‌اش نشنید. چیزی نگفت. لیوانش را بالا گرفت و دستش را روی نیم‌دایره‌یی در هوا چرخاند و همراه آن و، کمابیش روی همان خط سیر، نگاه چرخانید و گفت «سرخوش!» نگاهش به من نبود. به من نبود، هم، به‌هرصورت، که اگر هم بود حق هرکدام از آن دو بازیگر و بازی‌ساز، آن سه‌تای در هوا، زیادتر از من بود.

پرسید «شعر؟»

گفتم «خالص.»

پرسید «همان حافظ؟»

گفتم «نه، یکی دیگر.»

پرسید «کدام‌شون اول؟»

«اول؟»

My defiance was out of love, and also from reason. My reason said, "Don't bow and He will show His wrath." And with this wrath, we go head to head, and we are in each other's minds. We remain in a relationship with each other. In the heart of every believer or heretic, wittingly or unwittingly, we are together. Forever. Not like Your other angels who are just employees in Your office of Godliness. You tell Adam to do this, and I tell him, "Don't do that, but do as I tell you, the other way. Not the way He told you." This way, Mr. God, I am forever in battle with You. In fact, I am wrestling with You, permanently. Permanently, in a tussle with you.'"

When I grew silent, he waited a few seconds and then he burst out laughing.

"Yes, that is how we are!"

"It was not Satan that fell, it was Adam that ascended. Don't say the Fall, say the Ascension."

"With one poem."

"With this kind of poetry. Poetry. From this kind of poetry." And again, he was laughing, and said, "This is what genius is."

I asked, "Which poem?"

Maybe in his laughter, he didn't hear, for he said nothing. He raised his glass and moved his hand in a semicircle in the air and along with it, and on the same trajectory, he moved his gaze and said, "Cheers." His eyes were not on me. Not directed at me either. Anyway, even if it was, the two players and the playmaker, those three in heaven, deserved it more than I did.

He asked, "Poem?"

I said, "Pure [poetry]."

He asked, "By the same Hafez?"

I said, "No, someone else."

He asked, "Which one came first?"

"First?"

«زودتر. از حیث زمان. از حیث زمان کدام‌شون اول؟»

گفتم «او زودتر بود. از او زودترها هم بودن، چندتای دیگه. درهرحال، هوای دیگه داره حافظ. ظریف‌تره. رنده.» رند را به فارسی آورده بودم، که نفهمید.

پرسید «رند؟»

گفتم «رند. یه لغت که نظیرش را ندیده‌ام که داشته باشین شما، عیناً.»

پرسید «یعنی چه؟ ظریف؟ ظریف‌تر؟»

گفتم «ظریف‌ترِ چندپهلوئی. مطلق‌گوتر. یه جور ابستره درکمال‌دقت، بُرنده‌تر بودن، عصاره‌گیر، زیبا از راه اشاره، از راهِ نگفتن، با نگفتن گفتن، با نکردن کردن.»

گفت «اینا تمام خودشون مطلقن، ابستره. ما هر دو داریم یه چیز می‌گیم.»

گفتم «شاید می‌رسیم به حرف من، کم‌کم. جور دیگه‌یی لغت ندارم من برای این تعریف. اشکال کار ابستره‌گفتن هم اینه، خودش، دیگه بگیریم همین ورورفتن به مفهوم‌ِمقادر برابر یك شكاك. فرمانِ قاطع یك قادر که حاجت نداره برای فهمیدن. حاجت نداره چون فکر می‌کَنیم — یا از روی بی‌فکری خیال می‌کنیم که خودش فهمه. فهمی که ثابته چون حاجت نداره به جنبیدن برای بیش‌ترفهمیدن. ثابته برابر جنبنده، ثابته برابر کوشنده. ثابته برابر جست‌وجوکننده و پرسنده، فهمی رودرروی تعقل و سنجیدن. بنابراین هر تعقل و سنجش، هر کوششی برای فهم بیش‌تر، می‌شه یه جور رودرروئی با او، می‌شه درافتادن با وضع و مقام و موضع او. هه! پس سئوال موقوف! راحت می‌خوای باشی، عاقبت‌به‌خیر می‌خواهی باشی؟ —سئوال

"Earlier, in terms of time. Which one was the first chronologically?"

I said, "He was earlier. But there were others who came earlier too, several others. Though Hafez is something else. He is more intricate. He is a *rend*." I said rend in Persian, and he had not understood.

"*Rend?*"

"*Rend*. A word for which I have not seen an equivalent in English. Or not exactly."

He asked, "What do you mean by 'intricate'? Intricate? More intricate?"

"More intricate in being more multilayered, more talking in absolutes, a kind of abstraction that is perfect in its precision, more incisive, more capable of capturing the essence, of expressing beauty by way of allusion, by way of not saying, saying by not saying, doing by not doing."

He said, "These are all themselves absolutes, abstractions. We are both saying the same thing."

I said, "Maybe we arrive at what I've been saying, little by little. I have no other way of describing this. That's the problem of speaking in abstractions; take, for example, this playing around with the concept of the Almighty going head-to-head with a skeptic. The absolute commandment of an Almighty has no need to be understood. It does not need it because we think or, in not thinking, we imagine that [the commandment] is itself thought. A form of cognition that is absolute because it requires no effort for better comprehension, absolute in the face of any interrogation, in the face any active inquiry; a cognition that is absolute in the face of any inquirer or interrogator; a form of cognition that defies reasoning or critique. As a result, any reasoning or critique, any effort to better understand, becomes a kind of confrontation with Him, becomes a challenge to His status, His place and standing. Thus questioning is forbidden. You want to live comfortably, you want to have a happy ending,

نکن اصلاً. هرچی گفته بگو چشم و قبول کن و از جات تکون نخور. حالا پس چرا ساخت و پس چرا قوهٔ تعقل داد، اگر که عالِم. یا اصلاً چه‌جور هم به چه‌کس گفت و کی می‌گه که به او گفت و کی می‌گه اون که گفت که به من گفت اشتباه نکرد و به‌جا و درست و بی‌اشتباه گفت، عیناً؟ حق این سئوال هم نیست؟ نه. نیست. خُب، این سئوال هم نیست. حق این سئوال هم نیست؟ نه. نیست. خُب، این می‌شه؟ نه. نمی‌شه. تعقل و سنجیدن می‌شه از شیطان، از کارهای شیطانی.»

گفت «خُب؟»

«همین.»

«حافظ چی؟»

«حافظِ هشیارِ رند حکایت خلقت را جور دیگه‌یی گفته. آورده‌تش در محیط شخصی معمولیش، محیط عادی روزانه‌ش — یا درواقع محیط شبانه‌ش.»

«اِه؟»

«نه از آن‌جورهاش.» و گفتم «گفته دیشب دیدم فرشته‌ها اومدن توی میکده، در زدن اومدن تو. و با شراب گِل آدم را خمیر کردند. اندازه را با هم جام گرفتند.»

«همین؟»

«همین.»

«جدی؟»

«حتماً.»

«واقع، همین؟»

«همین. گفتم. گفتم که با نگفتن گفتن.»

فکری کرد و گفت «یعنی آدم را از شراب و خاک درست کردن، از پیش‌پاافتاده‌ترین مایه‌های خشک مخلوط با والاترین مایع محرک احساس و فکر.»

then don't ask any questions, at all. Whatever He has said, say yes and accept it, and don't make any effort of your own. But then why did He create and why did He confer on us the power of reasoning, if indeed He is the one who conferred it? Only God knows. What is more, how and to whom did He talk, and who is it who claims He talked to him, and who can guarantee that the one who claims He talked to him did not make a mistake and repeated [His words] accurately and completely and without error? Exactly? No right to even ask this question. The right to ask any question does not exist. No right. None. Well, can this work? No, it can't. Reasoning and analysis belong to Satan, become Satanic work."

"And so?"

"That is it."

"What about Hafez?"

"The clever *rend* Hafez has rendered the story of creation in another way. Has rendered it in the context of his normal personal environment, the environment of his normal everyday life—or his nocturnal environment."

"Oh!"

"Not of that sort." And then I added, "He has said that last night he saw angels come to the tavern, they knocked on the door and came in. And with wine they turned Adam's mud into clay, and they used wine cups for measuring."

"That is it?"

"That is it."

"Really?"

"Really, that is it?"

"That's it. I told you, saying by not saying."

He thought a bit and said, "Meaning they made Adam from wine and mud, from combining the most common dry matter with the most sublime liquid that inspires sensation and thought."

صبر کردم که باز بگوید تا بلکه بیش‌تر بگوید ولی در انتظار من را نگاه می‌کرد. گفتم «یه‌کمی بیش‌تر، بالاتر از این، یك‌کم.»

«چه؟»

«رپورتاژه. گزارش می‌ده.»

خیره هم‌چنان به من نگاه می‌کرد.

گفتم «گزارش می‌ده. در ابتدای کارِ خلقتیم. آدم هنوز آفریده نیس. دارن می‌سازنش اون‌جا. حافظ، ولی، اون‌جاس. شاهدِ همون لحظهٔ شروع آفرینش آدم، از یك طرف فرشته‌ها هسن، سرگرمِ گِل خمیرکردن و قالب‌زدن، با شراب و جام، البته، که البته نکتهٔ اساسی این شعر و حرف ما نیس این. اینه که شاعر آن‌جا بود. در ابتدای خلقت اون‌جا بود. می‌دید. دید. اون‌چه را که پیش می‌آمد دید. آدم نبود هنوز آفریده، او هم نبود فرشته. او نه فرشته بود نه آدم.»

«شیطان بود. شیطان بود؟»

«شیطانْ شیطان نبود هنوز اون‌وقت. شیطان فرشته بود هنوز، اون‌وقت، مقرب بود. میان دیگر فرشته‌ها یکی هم او. فرشته، فقط، مثل دیگرون. نه را نگفته بود هنوز، اون‌وقت، سئوال نکرده بود هنوز اون‌وقت.»

می‌دیدم از میانهٔ حرفم چشم‌هاش جمع‌تر شد. گفت «اِه!»

گفتم «آره.»

گفت «پیچیده‌تر از اون یکی دیگه‌س، انگار. آره؟»

گفتم «مطلق‌تر، به‌هرصورت. خلاصه‌تر، مقطرتر، پرورده‌تر، جاافتاده‌تر. ترسیده‌تر، شاید. از زور ترس جاافتاده‌تر، شاید. هم‌چنین بلندنظرتر؛ سرواننده‌تر، با قناعت و مناعت طبع زیادتر. در گفتن و در ساختن.»

پرسید «اون یکی کی بود، گفتی؟»

I waited for him to speak, maybe say something more, but he continued to look at me in anticipation. I said, "A little more to it than this, just a bit."

"What?"

"It is reportage. He is reporting."

Bewildered, he continued to look at me.

I said, "He is reporting. We are at the moment of creation; Adam is yet to be created. They are creating him right there. Hafez, however, is already there. The witnesses to the moment of creation are the angels, busy making clay and fashioning molds, with wine and wine glasses, of course. And of course, the pivotal point of the poem and of our conversation is not this. It is that the poet was there. He was there at the moment of creation. He saw. He was there. He witnessed what happened. Adam had not yet been created and he was not yet an angel. He was neither an angel nor Adam."

"Satan was there. Satan was there?"

"Satan was still not Satan yet. Satan was an angel still. He was beloved. One among the many angels. An angel only, like the others. He hadn't yet said no at this point, he hadn't yet questioned [God's authority] at that time."

I could see his eyes narrowing as I talked. He said, "Wow!"

"Yes.'

"It is a more complicated poem than the other, apparently. Yes?"

I said, "More absolute, anyway. More pithy. More purified, more developed, more matured, more fearful maybe. More matured from fear, maybe. Also loftier in vision, more defiant, with greater confidence and more dignity, both in speaking out and in creating."

He asked, "Who was the other, did you say?"

نگفته بودم هنوز. گفتم «یه دوافروش. دواساز بود.»

نگاهش می‌گفت انگار که شك دارد كه من راست می‌گویم. به‌طعنه در همان هوای شك پرسید «اسم نداشت او؟»

گفتم «چه‌طور نداشت؟ البته داشت. عطار بود اسمش.»

پرسید «ایرانی بود؟»

گفتم «این حرف‌ها نبود اون‌وقت. مملكت نبود اون‌وقت، این از همان ابستراکسیون‌هاس خودش. اسمی هم نبود ازش اصلاً. اسمی نداشت، اصلاً. مردم اهل ده و شهرشون بودن. آدم‌های مثل او ـ اهل عقیده‌شون، فكرشون.»

کمی در سکوت ماند. من هم گذاشتم که بماند. بعد گفت «هرجا همین‌جور بوده، یه‌وقت. از حیث مملكت، یعنی. مردم تابع قلدرِ محلیِ قاپنده، یا به‌ارث‌رسیده‌یی بودند، ما شاید هم بدتر؟ یا شاید هم بهتر، چون جزیره‌یی هستیم. که رفت‌وآمد بیگانه در جزیره کم‌تر بود.»

گفتم «بیگانگی از این‌ور یا اون‌ور یه‌خط‌بودن می‌آد، مگر؟»

شاید نشنید، شاید قبول داشته بود که این‌جور است؛ یا شاید فکرش جای دیگر بود.

پرسید «کی، در چه سالی بود؟»

گفتم «سال درستش یادم نیس. یه ده ـ بیست ـ سی‌سالی از قرن سیزدهم رفته وقتی که شهرش مسخر مغول‌ها شد، که کشتندش.»

«کشتندش؟»

«کشتندش. هشتادساله بود، چیزی در این حدود، که کشتندش. آره، کشتند.»

«پیرمرد را؟ پیرمرد را چرا کشتند؟»

«سگ‌ها و گربه‌ها را هم کشتند.»

«شاعر؟ شاعر را چرا کشتند؟»

I hadn't yet said who it was. I said, "A pharmacist, a pharmacologist."

His eyes said that he doubted that I was telling the truth. With sarcasm, and in a skeptical tone, he asked, "He had no name?"

I said, "How could he not have? Of course he did. Attar was his name."

He asked, "Was he an Iranian?"

I said, "No such language at that time; no such country at the time. This itself is one of those abstractions. There was no mention of it even. It had no name, at all. People were named after their village or city; people like him were labeled by what they believed, what they thought."

He remained silent for a while. I decided to let him be. Then he said, "It was the same everywhere, at one time. On the issue of the country, that is. People were subjects of a local bully who had grabbed power or inherited it, or probably worse. Or maybe better, because we are an island and in our case there was less movement of strangers."

I said, "Do you think being a stranger comes from being from this or that side of a line?"

Maybe he didn't hear, or maybe he agreed that it is indeed this way, or maybe his mind was elsewhere. He asked, "When, in what year was it?"

I said, "The exact year I don't remember. It was ten to twenty years into the thirteenth century when his city was conquered by the Mogols, and they killed him."

"They killed him?"

"They killed him. He was eighty, or thereabouts, when they killed him. Yes, they killed him."

"The old man? Why did they kill the old man?"

"They even killed dogs and cats."

"Poet? Why did they kill the poet?"

»اگر دونسته بودن که شاعره شاید هم زیادتر می‌کشتندش.«

»جدی؟«

»خیلی. شوخی ورنمی‌داره قتل‌عام و جنگ. قتل‌عام بود، سوا نمی‌کردند. "وی تو"[20] روی لندن شما سوا می‌کرد؟ سوا می‌کنن اصلاً؟ آپولینر،[3] ویلفرد اُون،[4] جدی شک دارین، راسی؟ کاونتری،[5] درسدن،[6] هیروشیما.[7] "تک‌شاخ‌های شَرِّ تمام را تاراندند"«

جا خورد. باز یک سطر شعر خودش بود که خودبه‌خود به ذهن و زبانم رسیده بود. نگاه تند ثاقبی به من می‌کرد، حس کردم خوشش نبود که باز از خودش شاهد آوردم. آخر انگار تاب نیاورد، پرسید »خودتان را آماده کرده بوده‌اید؟«

اول درست نفهمیدم؛ بعد از لای نگاه خیره‌یی که به من می‌کرد فهمیدم چه می‌گوید. دیدم پرت می‌گوید. پی بردم به کج‌رفتن گمان نادرستِ نابه‌جاش. صد سال هم اگر کسی سئوال ازم می‌کرد که این شعرش را به خاطر دارم یا بتوانم آن را به یاد بیاورم، نه، نداشتم، نمی‌آوردم، نمی‌آمد. اما اکنون حضور خودش همراه با روند حرف‌هامان آن شعر را سُرانده بود به ذهنم، به زبانم رسانده بود بی آن‌که ملتفت باشم که ممکن است هوش تند او بیامیزد به وسوسه بدگمانی بیگانه‌بودنش، به آسیب‌گیربودن احساس و شور یک شاعر، واقعاً شاعر. از شعرهای او، به هر شماره و اندازه‌یی که بود من تنها برخورد کرده بودم به چندتائی در ماهنامهٔ هورایزن که مجموعه‌اش را عزیز حاتمی هدیه داده بود به من، و هم‌چنین به پنج ـ شش‌تائی در یک جُنگ از شعرهای معاصر که اسکار ویلیامز[8] گرد آورده بود، و از میان

"If they had known he was a poet, they would have killed him more."

"Seriously?"

"Absolutely. Massacres and wars are nothing to joke about. It was a massacre. They didn't pick. The V2 over your London picked? Do they ever pick? Apollinaire, Wilfred Owen? Do you really doubt it? What about Coventry, Dresden, and Hiroshima? 'And the unicorn evils run them through.'"[20]

He was shocked. It was again a line of his poetry that had come to my mind of its own accord and rolled off my tongue. He gave me a sharp and piercing look. I felt he didn't like that I had provided testimony from him. Finally he could apparently bear it no more and asked, "Had you prepared yourself?"

Initially I didn't quite understand, then from the piercing look he gave me I understood what he had meant. I realized he was just off. I understood the root of his wrong and rude conclusion. If, out of nowhere, someone had asked me whether I remembered this poem of his, or could recollect it, I would have said, no, I don't remember, can't recollect, it won't come to mind. But now his presence, along with the contour of our conversation, had slid the poem into my mind and put it on my tongue, and I had not noticed that his sharp intellect might combine with the mistrustful inclinations of a stranger, and with the emotional and exuberant vulnerabilities of a poet, a real poet. From his poems, however many and however long they were, I had encountered only a few in the *Horizon* monthly magazine whose entire collection Aziz Hatemi had presented to me as a gift and I had also read five or six of his poems in a collection of modern poetry compiled by Oscar Williams,[21] and from all

---

20. From Thomas's "And death shall have no dominion," written in 1933.

21. Oscar Williams, *A Little Treasury of Great Poetry: English & American, from Chaucer to the Present Day* (New York: C. Scribner's Sons, 1946).

همین شعرهایی که به چشمم رسیده بود تنها، تصادفی، چند سطر پراکنده جا گرفته بود در ذهنم، در گوشه‌های حاشیهٔ ذهن، که چندان هم خبر نداشتم از بودنشان در ذهن. اما اصلاً چه عیب داشت اگر واقعاً چنین اتفاق افتاده بود که از پیش دانسته باشم که به او برخورد خواهم کرد و از پیش خود را آماده کرده باشم برای چنین برخورد، و چندتا از مشخصه‌هایش را و از آن‌جمله چندسطری هم از شعرهاش را به یاد نگاه داشته باشم تا در گفت‌وگوی احتمالی و حتی دورتر از احتمال در آینده‌ام با او آماده یا آماده‌تر باشم؛ عیبی نداشت این، چه عیبی داشت؟ و به‌هرحال اکنون چنین هم اتفاق نیافتاده بود و من آسان می‌توانستم از سر این گفته‌اش بگذرم، و اشتباه بی‌اهمیت او را به جوششی که شعرهاش به من داده بود ببخشم. تنها با تکان سر بهش گفتم نه، و با تکان دست به پیشخدمت که دور بود اشاره‌یی کردم که بیاید و آبجو بیاورد. لیوان من هم‌چنان پر بود.

کمی در سکوت ماندیم. بعد گفت «یک‌کم از آن دوافروش بخوانید.»

حس کردم می‌خواهد راضیم کرده باشد و نوعی عذر خواسته باشد از چیزی که فکر می‌کند مرا رنجاند. نرنجیده بودم من. آسان می‌توان از غریبه نرنجید. رنجیدن از خودی است، همیشه. از توقع است و از غریبه توقعی نیست. توقعی نباشد، اگر، از چه رنجیدن، از که رنجیدن، چرا رنجش؟ گفتم «به صورت شعری چیزی از او به یاد ندارم، مگر چند سطر پراکنده. یا یکی که، تازه، فقط حدس می‌زنم از او باشد. که شاید نباشد هم اصلش از قصه‌های یونانی است.»

پرسید «یونان؟ چرا یونان؟»

گفتم «از این اتفاقات می‌افته.» و بعد برایش گفتم تمدنشان در تمدن ما راه پیدا کرد، خاصه در اوایل دوران اسلامی. گفتم «برجسته‌های مردمی که ازآن‌پیش زیر سلطهٔ ساسانیان بودند عامل نقل و نفوذ بخشی از تفکر و از دانش یونان و آن‌ها را به یک زبان انعطاف‌پذیر محکمی درآوردند که سلطه می‌گرفت بر قلمرو پهناوری که در ظاهر به نیروی آیین و ربط نو یکی می‌شد، هرچند هم که درظاهر.»

I had read, only a few lines, by accident, here and there, had clung to my memory, in a marginal corner of my mind, and I was not all that aware of their existence in that isolated corner. But what was the problem if in fact I had prior knowledge of my encounter with him, and had studied some of his personal traits and a few lines of his poetry to be prepared, or more prepared, for my conversation with him, or even the more remote possibility of a future encounter? There was no problem—what was the problem? Anyway, nothing like this had happened and I could easily ignore his words or forgive his insignificant error in recognition of the effervescence I felt in his poetry. Only with the nod of a head I told him no, and with a gesture of my hand, I summoned the waiter, who was far away, to come and bring us more beer. My glass was still full.

We remained silent for a while. He said, "Recite a bit from that pharmacist."

I felt he wanted to console me and offer something of an apology for what he thought had hurt me. I wasn't hurt. It is easy not to be hurt by a stranger. You get hurt by someone you know, always. It is from expectation and there is no expectation from a stranger. With no expectation, there is nothing to be hurt about, who would be hurting you, why would you be hurt? I said, "I can't remember anything of his poetry, except some scattered lines. Or even one that I just think might be by him, and maybe the original is not his, but from fragments in Greek.

He asked, "Greek? Why Greek?

I said, "Things like this happen." And then I told him their civilization had found a way into ours, particularly in the early Islamic period. I said, "The elite of those who had earlier been under Sasanian rule became agents for the transmission and dissemination of Greek ideas and knowledge, and they rendered them into a more flexible and enduring language, one that could expand into a vast domain that was becoming dominated by the force of the new faith and new relations, albeit only in appearance."

گفت «یونان پاگان چندخدائی و اسلام؟»

برایش گفتم که سده‌های اجتماعی قدیم با روی‌کارآمدن نظم دین نو
افتاد؛ سواد‌داشتن از قید رسم خاصِ «کاست» از انحصار دستهٔ روحانی و
دبیر و کارمند دفترودستک‌های دیوانی درآمد و هوش و قریحه‌ها به افق‌های
تازه رو آورد، و مردم تلک‌تلک می‌آمدند، اما می‌آمدند، توی شعر و فهم و
فکرکردن‌ها، سواد و دانش‌ها. دین به توسعهٔ فکر کاری نداشت چون کوشش
پیروزمندانه‌اش بر این نفع بود و غنیمت. کاری نداشت اگر هم مخالفت
نداشت. از پیشرفت دین تازه که دیوارهای دورهٔ پیشین تَرَک برداشت، نور
تفکرِ تازه از شکاف تَرَک‌ها به تو آمد.

Horizon .۱

۲. ۲V، سلاح موشکی آلمان در جنگ جهانی دوم.

۳. هنرشناس و هنرمند و شاعر برجستهٔ فرانسوی (از اصل لهستانی و ایتالیائی)
که چند روز پیش از پایان جنگ جهانی اول به کشتن رفت.

And the unicorn evils run them through;.۴

۵. شهر انگلیسی که در جنگ دوم چنان به ضرب بمب‌های نیروی هوائی
آلمان ویران شد که کلمه «کاونتری ـ شده» و «کاونتریدن» در زبان‌های
اروپائی به وجود آمد.

۶ شهر قدیمی و زیبای آلمانی که بی داشتن ارزش و هدف نظامی، تنها به قصد
انتقام، از بمب‌های آتش‌زای نیروی هوائی انگلیس ویران شد.

۷. شهر ژاپنی که با اولین بمب اتمی آمریکا یک‌سره نابود شد.

Oscar Williams, *A Little Treasury of Great Poetry: English* .۸
& American from Chaucer to the Present Day.

He said, "The pagan, polytheist Greece and Islam?"

I told him that the old social barriers fell with the advent of the order of the new religion, and literacy was freed from the traditions and shackles of the "caste" and was no longer the monopoly of a group of clerics and scribes and bureaucrats in state offices and such, and intelligence and talent sought new horizons, and people would come, initially one by one, but they came to poetry and to new ideas, to literacy and to knowledge. Religion had no truck with expansion of thought, because the victory of its struggle was predicated on its benefits and the opportunities it could provide. It didn't bother with it, even if it did not oppose it. From the growth of the new religion, the old walls of the ancient regime cracked, and the light of new ideas entered through these cracks.

Dylan Thomas with his wife Caitlin.

THEIR MAN IN ABADAN

DYLAN THOMAS IN IRAN

Abbas Milani *&* Alina Utrata[1]

In 1951, when the Anglo-Iranian Oil Company sent him to
Iran, Dylan Thomas was on thin ice—both intellectually and
emotionally. His addiction to what James Joyce might have
called "riots of libidinous emotion" had once again frayed his
already fraught relationship with his wife, Caitlin. In his letters
from Iran, this tangled web of emotions, and his continuously
dire financial situation, were his main preoccupations. The price
and paucity of beer and whiskey and vodka were, of course,
another recurring theme. The business and politics of oil, for
which he was hired and sent to Iran, registers little.

Dylan Thomas was on even thinner intellectual ice about
Iran. His encounter with Ebrahim Golestan is a stark reminder of
his profound ignorance about the country. His letters and the few
pages of notes he wrote in his journal while in Iran,[2] as well as
his contributions to a BBC radio program, all show how little he
knew about the country—and how little he tried to learn. Other

---

1. Alina Utrata is a Ph.D. candidate in Politics and International
   Studies at the University of Cambridge and a Gates Cambridge
   scholar.
2. Dylan Thomas Journal, Jeff Towns (Dylan Thomas) Collection
   D1/1/5, National Library of Wales.

than a passing reference to Edward FitzGerald's translation of Omar Khayyam's *Rubaiyat* in his conversation with Golestan (p. 69), he exhibits almost no knowledge of the country. His letters only confirm this ignorance. In his contribution to the BBC broadcast, there is a reference to Persepolis, but he was and remained ignorant about Iran's rich cultural heritage and poetry, the contested role of Britain in modern Iranian politics, and the dynamics of the unfolding epic encounter between Iran and Britain over the question of oil. His enigmatic but poignant last words in the BBC broadcast—"Oil's oily. And the poor are waiting"[3]—is the only reference to the critical geopolitical issue that would underpin the Iranian oil nationalization crisis only a year later.

Of abject poverty in Iran, Thomas waxed eloquent in his letters. Of the role the Anglo-Iranian Oil Company and its greed that played a role in perpetuating this poverty, he was deafeningly silent. A friend noted that Thomas

> was very amused at the idea of his having been sent to Persia to report on the marvelous things that were being done for the people of Persia in the way of schools, hospitals and so forth by the oil company who were responsible for it, and at the same time horrified at the condition under which the Persian people were living … He came back [from Iran] writhing with indignation, but this, of course, only lasted until he was indignant about something else, or delighted about something else.[4]

Thomas was by then a celebrity poet in much of the English-speaking world, considered a "progressive" intellectual. In Iran,

---

3. Dylan Thomas, *Dylan Thomas: The Filmscripts*, ed. John Ackerman (London: J.M. Dent, 1995), p. 242.
4. Alban Leyshon to Colin Edwards, in David N. Thomas (ed.), *Dylan Remembered: Volume Two 1935–1953* (Bridgend, Wales: Seren, 2004), p. 175.

by contrast, he was all but unknown. Still, Ebrahim Golestan—
who was even then known for his impressive cosmopolitan
erudition—had heard of Thomas. He could quote lines of the
Welshman's poetry to him from memory, much to Thomas's
mistrustful surprise. However, it would be nearly a decade after
Thomas's journey before one of his works—a gothic short story
called "The Mouse and the Woman"—would be translated into
Persian. And it was another three decades before a translated
collection of Thomas's poetry was published in Iran.[5]

To some Western literary critics and anthologists, Thomas is
considered to be one of the great poets of the English language.[6]
His power of oratory and his ability to read poetry—his own,
as well as others'—are said to have been mesmerizing. During
a poetry reading by Thomas in Tehran organized by the British
Council, one attendee commented, "He read so beautifully
that I was shivering with delight. I had that delightful sensation up one's spine, when a reading is so beautiful ... that one
shivers with joy ... It was a memorable experience."[7] The great
composer Igor Stravinsky was so taken by one of Thomas's
performances that he invited him to visit California to work
together on an opera. In the months before his untimely death,

---

5. Dylan Thomas, "*Moush v zan*" [The Mouse and the Woman],
   trans. Mehrdad Samadi, *Ketab Hafteh*, 91 (September 8, 1963 [17
   Shahrivar 1342]), pp. 4–21. Fuad Naziri translated a collection of
   Thomas's poetry in 2015, published by Salés Publishers in Tehran.
6. As Golestan explains in "Encounter with Dylan Thomas," he had
   read some of Thomas's poetry in one of these collections (p. 111).
   See, for example, Oscar Williams, *A Little Treasury of Modern
   Poetry: English & American* (New York: Scribner, 1950), and
   idem, *Immortal Poems of the English Language: British and
   American Poetry from Chaucer's Time to the Present* Day (New
   York: Washington Square Press, 1952). Since then, many other
   anthologies have included Thomas in the pantheon of great poets.
7. David N. Thomas, *Dylan Thomas: A Farm, Two Mansions and a
   Bungalow* (Bridgend, Wales: Seren, 2000), p. 156.

Thomas's consolation and hope of financial relief hung on the possibility of this collaboration.[8] He had also dabbled in making documentaries, writing anti-fascist and anti-Nazi scripts during the Second World War for the British government.

In 1951, just as Iran was engaged in a major political war with the British, Thomas was commissioned by the rapacious Anglo-Iranian Oil Company for another propaganda film, this time about Iran. Not long after his visit, the company would become the flashpoint for a nationalization crisis that continues to affect the politics and historical trajectory of Iran today.

It was not the last time the West would send a cultural celebrity to Iran in a moment of crisis, nor even a celebrity who knew nothing about the country. In 1979, Michel Foucault was similarly sent to Tehran to "cover" the Iranian Revolution, becoming bizarrely, albeit briefly, enamored with the theocratic regime in the process. Dylan Thomas, at least, had no illusions about why he was there. Immediately after returning to England, he confided to a friend:

> the Anglo-Iranian Oil Company sent me out to write
> a film script to show how beautiful Persia is and how
> little as a mouse and gentle is the influence there of
> that Company: My job was to help pour water on
> troubled oil. I got out just before martial law ... and
> perhaps, disguised, will be sent back to write a script
> to show, now, suddenly, how beastly Persia is and how
> grandly irreplaceable is that thundering Company.[9]

Thomas was not wrong: the film was first and foremost a propaganda project by the Anglo-Iranian Oil Company, which

---

8. His letters in 1953, the year of his death, are replete with references to this possibility. See Paul Ferris (ed.), *Dylan Thomas: The Collected Letters* (London: J.M. Dent, 2000), p. 992.

9. Ferris (ed.), *Dylan Thomas: The Collected Letters,* p. 882.

company executives claimed would be "one of the most important publicity projects ever undertaken by the company" and "the first genuine effort to portray Iran sympathetically to the outside world."[10] As Mona Damluji has argued, historic relationships of colonialism were increasingly seen as illegitimate in the post-war order and thus the Anglo-Iranian Oil Company "had to justify its continuing practices of oil exploitation and extraction as a fundamental part of Britain's postcolonial civilizing mission, framed as a win-win situation wherein Iran exchanged its oil for the promise of modernity."[11] The film was thus part of the company's propaganda effort to justify why the British should be allowed to continue their extractive control over Iranian oil, demonstrating to the British public and Iran that the Anglo-Iranian Oil Company was "the benevolent harbinger of modernity in an otherwise backward country."[12]

The company chose Thomas to write the script, despite his lack of knowledge about Iran, presumably because they wanted a well-known broadcaster for such a public-facing film, as well as the fact that he was old friends with the director, Ralph Keene.[13] Thomas also needed the money. However, when Greenpark Productions finally released *Persian Story* in 1952, the scriptwriter was James Cameron, a British journalist, not Dylan Thomas.[14] Thomas never actually completed the script

---

10. Ronald Tritton, "Memo to Mr. Keating," February 6, 1951, 183091, BP Archive, and "Draft Memorandum to General Management and Chief Representative in Iran," 1950, 183091, BP Archive. Cited in Mona Damluji, "The Oil City in Focus: The Cinematic Spaces of Abadan in the Anglo-Iranian Oil Company's Persian Story," *Comparative Studies of South Asia, Africa and the Middle East, 33:1 (August 1, 2013)*, p. 75.
11. Damluji, "The Oil City in Focus," p. 82.
12. Ibid.
13. Thomas, *A Farm, Two Mansions and a Bungalow*, p. 165.
14. The film published by Greenpark Productions can be viewed at https://film.iwmcollections.org.uk/record/39799

he was hired to write. There are multiple theories as to why Thomas never completed the script, although it was likely due to some sort of relational breakdown between Thomas and the production company. We examine these theories in more depth throughout this essay. Some commentators have implied that Thomas was so disgusted by the poverty he saw in Iran that he could not bring himself to continue with the company's propaganda project. Others point out that the poet had a habit of not finishing commissioned scripts, especially ones for which he had already been paid. Still others have suggested that Greenpark Productions may have removed Thomas from the project themselves, either because of the poet's contribution to what the Anglo-Iranian Oil Company saw as an "unfavorable" BBC broadcast or because of filming difficulties after unrest in Iran forced them to change the project.[15] As Nariman Massoumi has noted, the original idea for the film was "based around a series of stories told in a Persian garden and scheduled to be filmed across the country," but filming ultimately became impossible due to protests and unrest across Iran.[16] Although it is difficult to say definitively what the Welshman's exact reasons were for not completing the script, what is known is that Thomas published nothing about his trip besides a short contribution to a BBC Radio broadcast. Indeed, because of this failure to produce anything of note—or perhaps because he seemed so intellectually unsuited to the mission—Thomas's visit to Iran has been shrouded in suspicion and allegations that he was actually a British spy.

Accusations of espionage and conspiracy are something of a leitmotif when it comes to the history of British involvement in Iran. Nevertheless, the main source of the rumor that Thomas was recruited by MI6 to gather intelligence about Iran seems to

---

15. Thomas, *A Farm, Two Mansions and a Bungalow*, p. 169. See also Thomas (ed.), Dylan Remembered, p. 175.
16. Naiman Massoumi, "Pouring Water on Troubled Oil: Dylan Thomas's Journey Through Iran," *Underline*, February 2018, 4–9.

have been an article by David Callard in the *New Welsh Review* in 1998.[17] Other British newspapers, including the *Guardian* and the *Daily Telegraph*, reported on the accusations in the Callard article when it appeared.[18] A day later, however, the Thomas biographer Paul Ferris wrote a letter to the editors of the *Guardian* to dismiss the espionage allegations as "barmy" and calling Thomas's Iran trip "about as mysterious as a glass of whisky."[19] Ferris believed that Thomas got the commission because Ralph Keene, the director and producer of the film, was an old friend. Years later, another Thomas biographer, David Thomas, no relation, conducted more substantial archival research into the allegations, but similarly concluded that while Dylan Thomas did indeed have many friends in British intelligence who could have recruited him, the accusation appears unfounded (although not impossible). As David Thomas pointed out, "If MI6 wanted to add to the information being gathered by their agents, they had available the large number of British people working in Iran … Why send a naïve, indiscreet, drunken poet?"[20]

Nevertheless, on January 8, 1951, the poet arrived in Tehran for what would be an unproductive visit. He was paid "probably two hundred fifty pounds, plus expenses."[21] In his first letter

---

17. According to Paul Ferris, the only proof David Callard had of the espionage claims was "a conversation, at an arts festival in 1980, with a poet who told him that in the 1950s he heard an elderly ex-spy, unnamed, say when drunk, 'Just look at that drunken fool, Dylan Thomas. We got to him in the end.'" Paul Ferris, *Dylan Thomas: The Biography* (Ceredigion, Wales: Y Lolfa, 2006), p. 297.
18. Michael Smith, "Dylan Thomas 'spied for MI6 on mission to Iran'," *Daily Telegraph*, January 1, 1999, and Richard Norton-Taylor, "Dylan Thomas: Tinker, Tailor, Poet, Spy?", *Guardian*, December 31, 1998.
19. Paul Ferris, "Letters to the Editor: Spies, Gongs and Eggs," *Guardian*, January 1, 1999.
20. Thomas, *A Farm, Two Mansions and a Bungalow*, p. 162.
21. Ferris, *Dylan Thomas: The Biography*, p. 257.

from Iran to his beloved, benighted, and by then beleaguered wife, Caitlin, there is little more than repeated protestations of unending love, and a desperate search for her forgiveness. He writes, "Caitlin my darling, dear, dear Caitlin, of my love so far away I love you. All these strange, lost days I love you, and I am lost indeed without you my dear wife."[22]

In his "Encounter with Dylan Thomas," Golestan more than once comments that Thomas behaved like a stranger in a strange land. The letters show much of the same spirit, indicating that he was probably not very engaged in learning more about Iran. For example, in his first letter, he writes how Iran "is so much further than America."[23] This distance was surely cultural and intellectual, rather than physical, as the actual distance between Iran and Wales is about the same as that between Wales and America. (Cardiff to New York is 3,333 miles; Cardiff to Tehran is 3,549 miles.)

The other theme of the letters is the issue of money and family finance—a problem he faced all his life as he tried to make a living as a poet. One critic has suggested that "from the age of twenty-three to his death at thirty-nine, [he] mentions money in every letter."[24] The first letter from Tehran continues with more emphatic declarations of love, even desperation. Thomas writes, "I do not know if you will ever love me again. And I'll die if you do not. I mean that."[25] Only in the last few lines does he even mention Tehran, writing in a brooding tone, "I have to go to see the town of Tehran which, at a quick look, seems depressing and half-made."[26] References to Tehran in his journal are all in the same vein.

---

22. Ferris (ed.), *Dylan Thomas: The Collected Letters*, p. 871.
23. Ibid.
24. Mathew Hodgart, "Old Pup," *New York Review of Books*, August 3, 1967.
25. Ferris (ed.), *Dylan Thomas: The Collected Letters*, p. 872.
26. Ibid.

Nearly sixty years before Dylan Thomas's visit, another British interlocutor, Gertrude Bell, traveled through Persia while visiting her uncle, the British minister in Tehran. While Bell would, of course, later go on to be an important spy, writer, archeologist, and "kingmaker" who shaped British imperial policy in the Middle East, the letters she wrote from Persia, at the age of twenty-four, and the book, *Persian Pictures*, that she published after her trip, were starkly different in both their tone and knowledge of Iran.[27] In one letter, she writes of her visit as "refreshing to the spirit," and of the beauty of the "trees of a Persian garden" and of reading the "the poems of Hafiz in the original" from "a book curiously bound in stamped leather" that she had bought in the bazaar, and was reading in a Zoroastrian garden, with its murmuring stream.[28] This idyllic image, displaying knowledge and interest in Persian culture, could not be further from Thomas's letters, with their disdain for Iran and a decided effort to remain ignorant. "Cat dear ... in the snow & the sun, understanding nothing of the savage town around, wanting to know nothing of ugly, dirty, dinning Tehran with mosques and sores and disease and Cadillacs." His description of his daily routine is no less disheartening: "I go with horrible oil-men to interview horrible government-men; I sit in the lounge of this posh Guest-House for horrible oil-men and listen to Scotch engineers running down the Persian wops."[29] These ethnic slurs litter his orientalist descriptions of the country, as he walks

> with a pleasant Persian guide through endless museums,
> palaces, libraries ... And my boredom bleeds ... Only
> the bazaar was wonderful ... Tehran bazaar, the largest in
> Persia—all the things one's read about ... one's ever seen,

---

27. Elias Muhanna, "What Gertrude Bell's Letters Remind Us About the Founding of Iraq," *New Yorker*, June 14, 2017.
28. Florence Eveleen Eleanore Olliffe Bell (ed.), *The Letters of Gertrude Bell* (Teddington, England: Echo Library, 2006), p. 14.
29. Ferris (ed.), *Dylan Thomas: The Collected Letters*, p. 874.

haggling and cursing and grinning and smelling everywhere
round one ... smelling of incense and carpets and food and
poverty. And women with only their eyes showing through
tattered, dirty, cobble-trailing thin black sack wraps ... and
lots of them with splayed and rotting high-heel shoes.

He writes of "beautiful dirty children in little chadurs" and of
the poor who wear "every kind of clothing, so long as it's dirty
and wretched." He observes—incorrectly—that the "only water
for the poor in Tehran ... runs down the public gutters. I saw an
old man pissing in the gutter, walking away a few years, then
cupping his hands and drinking from it. This running cesspool
is the only drinking and washing water for the poor."[30]

Thomas seems all but oblivious to the patriotic rage seething
throughout the country. The director Ralph Keene, with whom
he was traveling for the film, reportedly made "desperate phone
calls home, concerned about the safety of the crew members" due
to the tense political situation in the country.[31] Upon returning to
England, Keene was apparently so dissatisfied by what he had
shot—which was only of Anglo-Iranian Oil Company property
or aerial footage, due to safety concerns—that he demanded the
project be canceled. Meanwhile, Thomas remained stubbornly
impervious to these political tensions, meticulously reporting
how much beer he drank ("eight pints of beer: all lager") and how
much he was charged for each pint ("Six shillings for a bottle
of beer"), ending the letter with yet another protestation of love
to Caitlin: "I love you in this dry city. I love you everywhere."[32]
Here, then, is poetic flair and lexical prowess in the service of
conjuring a desolate image of Iran, bereft of all context and
nuance, knowledge, and humility. He blames the "oil men," but
it is not clear who these men are, or which master they served.

---

30. Ibid.
31. Thomas, *A Farm, Two Mansions and a Bungalow*, p. 166.
32. Ferris (ed.), *Dylan Thomas: The Collected Letters*, p. 874.

While, in his letters from the U.S., Thomas repeatedly refers
to his poetry readings, his letters from Iran strangely make no
mention of the poetry reading that had been organized for him
by the British Council in Tehran, attended by over a hundred
people and reportedly to much appreciation.[33]

The next letter was sent on January 16 from the city of
Ahwaz, in the oil-rich south of Iran. He again begins, at lumbering
and lingering length, to lament not receiving any letter from his
"darling dear" Caitlin, threatening that if indeed he did find out
that she has said, "he is dead to me," then he will "indeed ... be
dead." Still the image he offers of Iran focuses on the poverty
and is at times extremely patronizing. He mentions seeing "rows
and rows of tiny Persian children suffering from starvation" and
recounts the heart-wrenching story of a child left unattended
by his poor mother. He describes how, on his train ride from
Tehran to Ahwaz, at every station "children rushed up to the
train from the mud-hut villages: Three quarters naked, filthy,
hungry, and, most beautiful with smiles." He writes of sharing
his food with the needy children and of meeting a "man worth
30,000,000 pounds" from a "thousand crooked deals."[34] He does
not mention the nationality of this crook, but as the Anglo-Iranian
Oil Company was a British government entity, he must have
meant an Iranian. In placing the blame on such crooked men,
he in effect deflects any blame from the oil company and the
British government who were the biggest beneficiaries of the
monopoly held on Iranian oil. Thomas's descriptions of poverty
in the country may have been compelling—and perhaps even
heartfelt—but he failed to see the true cause of the injustice
around him, nor his own complicity in perpetuating it when

---

33. Reference to this reading can be seen in PRO, "British Council
    Archives, Annual Report," PER/701/3, 1948–1952, BW 49/10. See
    also a more detailed discussion in Thomas, *A Farm, Two Mansions
    and a Bungalow*, p. 156.
34. Ferris (ed.), *Dylan Thomas: The Collected Letters*, p. 875.

he agreed to make a propaganda film for the oil company. The dire poverty he writes about was in no small part a result of the Anglo-Iranian Oil Company's exploitative practices. And it was the crooked men of that company who were paying his way.

While Thomas's letter of February 16 is full of exhortations of love to his "Cat," the next day, upon his arrival in the city of Abadan where he encountered Golestan, he sent a letter not to Caitlin but to Pearl Kazin—the American journalist with whom Thomas had started an affair, the discovery of which had become the source of the latest strife with his wife. His marriage, which Caitlin Thomas had supposedly once described as "raw, red bleeding meat,"[35] was emotionally fraught and boozy, and littered with mutual affairs and public arguments, although also loving and passionate (they remained married until Dylan Thomas's death in 1953).[36] It is in the letter to Pearl, however, that Thomas most directly talks about his stay in Abadan. His language there is even more stunning in its orientalist disdain for what Winston Churchill would have called the "restive natives." While Thomas clearly quotes passages from his conversation with Golestan in the letter, he never mentions him by name.

In the letter to Kazin, the tired, pleading, anguished, dour tone of his letters to Caitlin is replaced with a more florid, poetic style. Poetry had after all brought him and Pearl together, and he was perhaps trying to keep the fire burning with more poetic prose. While Golestan in his conversation with Thomas, had tried to take Thomas on a cultural tour of Iran, the poet himself exudes the smug disposition of a First World tourist visiting a Third World shanty town. He declares he is writing from

---

35. "Caitlin Thomas, 81, Writer and Widow of Dylan Thomas Obituary," *The Associated Press*, August 2, 1994.
36. The turbulent but enduring nature of this complicated relationship has been covered in many books and articles and invariably plays a prominent role in any biography of Thomas. See, for example, Ferris, *Dylan Thomas: The Biography* (London: Phoenix, 1999).

a tasty, stifflipped, liverish, British Guest House in puking
Abadan on, as you bloody well know, the foul blue boiling
Persian buggering Gulf. And lost, God blast, I gasp between
gassed vodkas, all crude and crude fuel oil, all petroleum
under frying heaven, benzola, bitumen, bunkers and
tankers, pipes and refineries, wells and derrick, gushers
and supper-fractionator and [?Shatt]-el Arab and all.[37]

Of the British, he also writes with bitter disdain, which may
be as much a result of Welsh nationalism as any sympathy for the
people of Iran. His disdainful words for his countrymen come
with ample references to their sexual habits, and of course the
needy wanton ways of "native" Persian girls. The British, he
says, are "all quietly seething. Many snap in the heat of their
ingrowing sex and sun, and are sent back, baying, to Britain,"
only to be replaced by "fresh recruits, young well-groomed pups
with fair moustaches and briar pipes," who soon begin to chain-
smoke and "scream blue on arak, toss themselves trembly all
sleepless night in the toss-trembling bachelors quarters, answer
the three-knock at the midnight door, see before them in the hot
moonlight wetmouthed Persian girls from the bazaar." To make
sure the voyeuristic images and the insulting implications of
his parsimony in his allusions to the "wetmouthed Persian girls
from the bazaar" are clearly understood, he then writes of these
young British men being "shipped back also, packed full with
shame and penicillin."[38]

Of Shiraz—a city that came up more than once in his
encounter with Golestan—he writes, "O overgreen, gardened,
cypressed, cinema'd, oil-tanked, boulevarded, incense-and-armpit
cradle of Persian culture."[39] He complains that the city has "no

---

37. Ferris (ed.), *Dylan Thomas: The Collected Letters*, p. 876.
38. Ibid, p. 876–7.
39. Ibid.

nightlife. Shiraz sleeps at nine ... There is no night life here, the moon does what she does, vermin persist, camels sail, dogs defy, frogs gloat, snow-leopards drift ..." He also informs Pearl that beer "costs ten shillings a bottle, whiskey one pound a nip."[40]

The next letter is from Isfahan. By then, he had received the letter that he had so desired and dreaded from his Cat, which, "as it was meant to, made me want to die."[41] Thomas confesses that he moves "through these days in a kind of dumb, blind despair," in "a strange town in a benighted country," in a "hotel full of brutes."[42] His sentiments about his trip and about Iran are more clearly evident in his letter of April 12, 1951 to John Brinnin—the critic and agent who had organized his 1950 tour of the U.S. Much of the letter is about his continued financial difficulties. In one paragraph, he offers his views on his trip to Iran, vowing to never go back there again:

> No. Persia wasn't all depressing. Beautiful Isfahan & Shiraz. Wicked, pompous, oily British. Nervous, corrupt, and delightful Persian bloody bastards. Opium no good. Persian Vodka, made of beetroot, like stimulating sock-juice, very enjoyable. Beer full of glycerine and pips. Women, veiled, or unveiled ugly, or beautiful and entirely inaccessible, or hungry. The lovely camels who sit on their necks and smile. I shan't go there again. Still broke and in debt. I spent all the Persian money on beetroot vodka, glycerine beer, unveiled ugly women, and, as you conjectured, the camels, the camels, the camels are coming.[43]

Orientalism, they say, eroticizes, exoticizes, and dehumanizes the "Oriental Other." Thomas's narrative in these letters could be used as textbook examples of such narratives. In his "Encounter

---

40. Ibid.
41. Ibid.
42. Ibid.
43. Ibid, p. 887.

with Dylan Thomas," Golestan is endlessly courteous and kind to Thomas, affording him the politeness he thinks he deserves as a guest—and, more importantly, as a great poet. Thomas's tone in his letter contrasts sharply with Golestan's hospitality. Here, too, the contrast with Bell is inescapable. She once wrote of visiting a home in Persia in which "all the time your host was probably a perfect stranger into whose privacy you had forced yourself in this unblushing way. Ah, we have no hospitality in the west and no manners. I felt ashamed almost before the beggars in the street, they wear their rags with a better grace than I."[44]

Thomas left Iran, traveling back to London in April 1951. He did not publish the film script he had been sent to complete. Thomas had apparently produced "some sort of script" for Greenpark Productions, but the company's executives did not like it. A friend of Thomas said that he had expressed

> tremendous disappointment about the difficulties they'd
> been experiencing in connection with the film ...
> they were not happily received by the authorities ...
> probably the oil company people wanted to exhibit what
> they had done ... and I should imagine that Thomas
> and Co. wished to show the romantic side of the
> country ... which would be the charm for any poet.[45]

In addition, as unrest gripped Iran, the film crew faced considerable difficulties in filming, and production was halted ahead of schedule as the crew ultimately had to leave Iran.

Furthermore, Thomas had no financial incentive to complete the script when he returned to England. When someone suggested that Thomas might write a script for the BBC about Persia in 1951, a producer replied:

---

44. Bell (ed.), *The Letters of Gertrude Bell*, p. 14.
45. Thomas, *A Farm, Two Mansions and a Bungalow*, p. 169.

> I don't think Third [the BBC Third Programme] will
> commission any more scripts from him until he has
> finished the two or three which have already been
> commissioned for some time. Moreover, I imagine
> that Persia is a rather tricky subject as regards policy;
> and I understand that the Anglo Iranian Company have
> some kind of hold over what Dylan might say.[46]

This turned out to be prescient. While Dylan was later commissioned by the BBC to write a script entitled *A Poet Looks at Persia*, he never completed it. On a letter from the BBC Persian Section to Thomas, inquiring after the script that "had been commissioned some time ago," the editor scribbled, "Cancelled. He did not write it."[47] As his biographer David Thomas has noted, "Nothing sinister should be read into Dylan's failure to write; it was just one of many commissions that he did not complete."[48]

Instead, Thomas did contribute to a BBC broadcast entitled "Persian Oil" which the British Foreign Office called "disastrous" (and which may have played a part in why Greenpark Productions ultimately removed him from their propaganda film). BBC Sounds broadcast the "Persian Oil" report on the Home Service on April 17, 1951. There were several contributors to the program, of whom Dylan Thomas was only one. Much of the material was provided by a long list of other contributors—including the academicians Ann Lambton and Robin Zaehner, two of the most important masterminds behind the eventual decision of the British and U.S. governments to overthrow Iranian prime minister Mohammad Mosaddegh, who had spearheaded the

---

46. See Thomas, *A Farm, Two Mansions and a Bungalow*, p. 162.
47. Ibid., p. 163.
48. Ibid.

drive to nationalize Iran's oil.[49] Nevertheless, the British Foreign Office, Treasury, and Information Policy Department had all advised the BBC against the broadcast, with the Foreign Office going so far as to call a conference to "discuss with the media how news and programmes on Iran should be handled."[50] In the Foreign Office deliberations, it was decided that

> if the BBC could not be persuaded to stop the programme
> then it should confine itself to the performance and
> achievements of the Company in Persia, and it should
> not include any of the following subjects: a) the case for
> nationalization (since the BBC would presumably want
> to state both sides of the question) ... b) the strategic
> importance of Middle East oil and the part which the
> [Anglo-Iranian Oil Company] may play in a future war.
> c) Russian interest in Middle East oil. d) Soviet-United
> Kingdom/United States rivalry in the Middle East.[51]

The official at the Foreign Office added that "the Anglo-Iranian Oil Company agree with my views on the undesirability of

---

49. The script was written by Aidan Phillip and Reggie Smith. Contributors included Dylan Thomas, John Davenport, Robin Zaehner, Christopher Sykes, Ann Lambton, Edward Hodgkin, David Mitchell, E. Lawson Lomax, and A.H. Hamzavi. Aside from Lambton and Zaehner, the probably accidental presence of Christopher Sykes, a son of General Sykes—of Sykes and Pico fame—is interesting. A copy of the radio script and contributors was reviewed by the authors in Public Record Office, Information Policy Department, PG 13434/3, FO 953/1152.

50. While we reviewed the relevant Foreign Office and British Council documents, extensive archival research on the internal churning of the British establishment in reaction to the program has been conducted by David Thomas. See Thomas, *A Farm, Two Mansions and a Bungalow*.

51. Public Record Office, Information Policy Department, PG 134337/3, April 6, 1951, FO 953/1152.

this broadcast and have spoken to Mr. Barden who said he would discuss it 'through the usual channels'."[52] Furthermore, the media was advised to "stress the [Anglo-Iranian Oil] Company's latest offers to settle the dispute, as well as the enormous benefits which it had brought to Persia."[53] Despite the British government's agitation, the BBC broadcast did go ahead.

Thomas's contribution to the broadcast begins with a description echoing what he had heard from Golestan about the island of Abadan—that "there was nothing on that hot and hateful bone-dry blistering bank but some dates that nobody kept, and a few lizards who had nowhere to go. And some jackals … howling at the Euphrates and waiting for man."[54] The words may have had poetic flair, but the description is inaccurate. In fact, the luscious green of the island of Abadan, and the existence of a coastguard station, has been documented as early as the time of Ptolemy (d. 170 CE).[55] Golestan had described Abadan as desolate to Thomas because he had been referring to the visit by a Persian poet to Abadan almost a thousand years earlier, (p. 55) trying to give Thomas a slice of Iran's culture and history. Thomas, however, took the reference to Persian history and concocted from it his own poetic rendition of the "hateful" city of lost lizards that was now "a huge, tubed town, streamlined, and reeking new: A kind of cinema organ of a town, with its petrified refinery pipes playing, all oily day, on the bank of the boiling river."[56] Crucially, however, his poetic rendition parrots the company line that there would have been no oil or city of Abadan had there been no "British men's burden" of civilizing Iran. Indeed, the BBC program overall

---

52. Ibid.
53. Ibid.
54. Thomas, *The Filmscripts*, p. 242.
55. Naser-e Khosraw, *Nāṣer-e Khosraw's Book of Travels* (Albany, N.Y: Bibliotheca Persica, 1986).
56. Thomas, *The Filmscripts*, p. 242.

reflects a patronizingly colonial and orientalist mindset. Robin Zaehner, minutes after Thomas, complains that "the Persians are an ungrateful race. They thanked us little for democracy."[57] Iran is elsewhere described as "medieval."[58] Although we have no way of knowing whether Thomas knew what would be said in the other parts of the broadcast, he clearly understood the nature of his assigned role in the project.

Much of the rest of Thomas's words in the BBC broadcast is simply a repetition of the descriptions of the country he had earlier penned in his letters. He talks of beggars and bazaars, of poor hungry children, and of the one crying disabled child that caught his attention. He "asked the English sister why" the child was crying. The nun replied that

> His mother went out every day ... begging in the streets, and he was too weak to go with her and she was too weak to carry him. So she left him alone in her hovel. The hovel had a hole dug in the earth floor, where a fire always was; a heap of hot cinders ready for cooking. The child fell in the fire, face down and lay there all day burning until his mother came home at dusk. He'll get better, but he's lost one arm and all of his toes.[59]

Reading this passage, one cannot help but think that Thomas thought of the Anglo-Iranian Oil Company as the saintly sister out to "save" the abandoned child of Iran—never realizing how complicit she had been in what had caused the plight of the impoverished and neglectful mother in the first place.

---

57. Public Record Office, "Report to the People: Persian Oil," Information Policy Department, PG 13434/3, April 6, 1951, FO 953/1152, p. 19.
58. Ibid.
59. Thomas, *The Filmscripts*, p. 243.

Like the British foreign establishment, the Anglo-Iranian Oil Company was furious about the "disastrous" BBC broadcast. One has to wonder, however, what exactly they were so upset about: the program seemed almost entirely congruent with the company's aims and outlook. In fact, the scene Thomas painted was, almost verbatim, what Ronald Tritton, the director of public relations for the Anglo-Iranian Oil Company, had originally envisioned for the film. As Tritton had pitched:

> The film might start at midnight in the Refinery itself something full of noise and steam and heat to set the scene. This noisy production sequence could give way to the quiet of a hospital ward in the early hours with an English nurse soothing an ill and frightened Iranian girl. From there we might go, say at 5am to the dairy farm and the comfortable homely noise of milking cows ... Do you see what I am getting at?[60]

Thomas clearly did. And, although he does describe the poverty of Iran, he demurs in placing any blame at the feet of the oil company—even in the BBC radio broadcast. Instead, he describes a desolate, impoverished Persia where the only remotely hopeful place is "prosperous Abadan" which is "a community [that] lives at the end of a pipeline."[61] Just as Tritton had hoped for his propaganda film, the message of Thomas's radio broadcast seemed to be that the only hope for Iran was the oil company.

Ironically, the *Persian Story* film that the Anglo-Iranian Oil Company produced only aired after Iranian oil was nationalized. Mona Damluji has argued that while Anglo-Iranian Oil Company executives claimed "they were working to counter-act negative stereotypes of Iran ... by projecting images of Middle Eastern modernity," the film ultimately "glosses over the

---

60. Ronald Tritton, "Film about Abadan," March 9, 1949, 183091, BP Archive. Cited in Damluji, "The Oil City in Focus," p. 82.
61. Thomas, *The Filmscripts*, p. 243.

complex, dynamic, and troubled socioeconomic conditions that underpinned the role of AIOC in the production of lived space around the Abadan refinery and in the making of the city."[62] It is hard to see how Thomas's words did anything to counteract this impression.

Much of Golestan's discussion with Thomas was about the rich and complicated cultural poetic tradition of Iran, and the difficulties of translating poems (into English or any other language). Words, Golestan said, all have an emotional aura and an historical baggage. Even with the best of intentions, and even with intimate knowledge of the original language, they cannot easily be rendered or understood in another language. Thomas did not heed the meaning behind Golestan's words that understanding Iran and its encounter at that time with Britain required knowledge and tact, humility and humanity. Thomas had come to Abadan intent upon using the alchemy of his poetry to make a propaganda film for the oil company. Golestan was using his discourse on language and translation and his refences to the rich cultural heritage of Iran as a metaphor to underscore for Thomas the complicated web of policy and politics that was entangling Iran and Britain. He urged the Welsh poet to go gently and humbly into the fight. Thomas failed to heed the advice and ranted angrily—always poetic, but often irksome—about an encounter with a culture he knew little about. One critic wrote that Dylan Thomas was famous for "his early death, for debt and drink, for the ordeals we think the gods inflict on those they love."[63] Going to Iran to "pour water on troubled oil" was certainly one such infliction.

---

62. Damluji, "The Oil City in Focus," p. 87.
63. Karl Miller, "The Outlaw," *New York Review of Books*, April 6, 1978.

EBRAHIM GOLESTAN FILMOGRAPHY

Drama

Darya (The Sea), unfinished, 1962

Kastegari (Marriage Proposal), 15 minutes, 1964

Khesht va ayeneh (Brick and Mirror), 120 minutes, 1974

Asrar-e ganj-e darre-ye jenni (Mysteries of the Ghost Valley/ The Ghost Valley's Treasure Mysteries), 137 minutes, 1974

Documentaries

Az ghatreh ta darya (From a Drop to the Sea), 30 minutes, 1957

Cheshm andaz-ha (Landscapes), 1957–1962 (a series of six shorts, two of which are lost):

> *Meydan-e chah-e naft* (The Oil Wells
> of Aghajari), 14 minutes
> *Pishraft-e tarha-ye Gachsaran-Khark* (Progress
> of the Gachsaran-Khark Project), 20 minutes
> *Gardesh-e charkh* (The Turning Wheel), 15 minutes
> *Ab va atash* (Water and Fire), 17 minutes

Khaneh siah ast (The House is Black), 21 minutes, 1961, this film is directed by Forough Farrokhzad and produced by Golestan

Kharab abad (Broken-Down Village), 10 minutes, 1961

Ma adamim (We Are Humans), 10 minutes, 1961

Moj, marjan, khara (Wave, Coral, Rock), 40 minutes, 1961

Yek atash (A Fire), 25 minutes, 1961

Tapeh-ha ye marlik (The Hills of Marlik), 15 minutes, 1963

Kharman va bazr (The Harvest and the Seed), 28 minutes, 1965

Ganjineh-ha ye gohar (The Crown Jewels of Iran), 14 minutes, 1966

Namayeshgah-e bazargani (The Commercial Expo of Tehran), 45 minutes, 1967

EBRAHIM GOLESTAN
SELECTED BIBLIOGRAPHY[1]

WORKS IN ENGLISH BY EBRAHIM GOLESTAN

Golestan, Ebrahim. "Esmat's Journey." In *Stories from Iran: An Anthology of Persian Short Fiction from 1921–1991*. Edited by Heshmat Moayyad. Washington, D.C.: Mage Publishers, 1992, pp. 131–135

BOOKS IN ENGLISH MENTIONING EBRAHIM GOLESTAN

Dabashi, Hamid. "Mud Brick and Mirror." In *Masters and Masterpieces of Iranian Cinema*. Washington, D.C.: Mage Publishers, 2014, pp. 71–107.

Jahed, Parviz. "Ebrahim Golestan and Writing with a Camera." In *The New Wave Cinema in Iran: A Critical Study*. London: Bloomsbury Academic, 2022, pp. 137–53

Langford, Michelle. *Allegory in Iranian Cinema: The Aesthetics of Poetry and Resistance*. London: Bloomsbury Academic, 2019.

---

1. Selection of works by or on Ebrahim Golestan compiled by Alina Utrata.

Milani, Abbas. "Ebrahim Golestan." In *Eminent Persians: The Men and Women Who Made Modern Iran, 1941–1979.* 2 vols. Syracuse, N.Y. : Syracuse University Press, 2008, pp. 852–59.

―――. "King of Shadows: Ebrahim Golestan and the Question of Modernity." In *Lost Wisdom: Rethinking Modernity in Iran.* Washington, D.C.: Mage Publishers, 2004, pp. 125–39.

―――. "Ghost Valley." In *The Persian Sphinx: Amir Abbas Hoveyda and the Riddle of the Iranian Revolution.* New edition: Washington, D.C.: Mage Publishers, 2000, pp. 243–63.

Mottadeheh, Negar. "Crude Extractions: The Voice in Iranian Cinema." In *Locating the Voice in Film.* New York: Oxford University Press, 2017, pp. 227–40.

Naficy, Hamid. "The Statist Documentary Cinema and Its Alternatives." In *A Social History of Iranian Cinema.* Durham, N.C.: Duke University Press, 2011, pp. 78–24.

Vahabzadeh, Peyman. "Rebels on the Silver Screen." In *The Art of Defiance: Dissident Culture and Militant Resistance in 1970s Iran.* Edinburgh: Edinburgh University Press, 2022, pp. 260–97.

Yaghoobi, Claudia (ed.). "The Grotesque Sigheh/Sex Worker's Body in Golestan's 'Safar-e 'Esmat.'" In *Temporary Marriage in Iran: Gender and Body Politics in Modern Iranian Film and Literature.* Cambridge: Cambridge University Press, 2020, pp. 156–74.

ARTICLES IN ENGLISH ABOUT EBRAHIM GOLESTAN

Banifatemi, Malihe Al-sadat, and Behzad Barekat. "Cultural Context: A Comparative Study of Raymond Carver's Cathedral and Ebrahim Golestan's 'The Stream and the Wall and the Thirst.'" *Cumhuriyet Üniversitesi Fen Edebiyat Fakültesi Fen Bilimleri Dergisi,* 36:3 (May 13, 2015), pp. 1284–90.

Ghasemnejad, Atefeh, and Alireza Anushiravani. "The Early Literary Reception of Ernest Hemingway in Iran." *International*

Journal of Comparative Literature and Translation Studies, 6:1 (January 31, 2018), pp. 29–35.

Hillmann, Michael C. "The Modernist Trend in Persian Literature and Its Social Impact." *Iranian Studies*, 15:1/4 (1982), pp. 7–29.

Hosseini, Mostafa. "A Review of 'Asgari Hasankloo, Asgar. *Time and Its Men: A Critique of Ebrahim Golestan's Stories.*'" *Persian Literary Studies Journal*, 5:7/8 (October 22, 2016), pp. 55–8.

Khoshbakht, Ehsan. "The Prose-Poetry Cinema of Ebrahim Golestan." *Sight and Sound*, March 2022.

Nafici, Hamid. "Iranian Writers, the Iranian Cinema, and the Case of 'Dash Akol.'" *Iranian Studies*, 18:2/4 (1985), pp. 231–51.

Poudeh, Reza J., and M. Reza Shirvani. "Issues and Paradoxes in the Development of Iranian National Cinema: An Overview." *Iranian Studies*, 41:3 (2008), pp. 323–41.

Rosenbaum, Jonathan. "Before the Revolution." *Chicago Reader*, May 3, 2007.

Saeed-Vafa, Mehrnaz. "Ebrahim Golestan: Treasure of Pre-Revolutionary Iranian Cinema." *Rogue Publishing*, 2007.

Sprachman, Paul. "Ebrahim Golestan's *The Treasure*: A Parable of Cliché and Consumption." *Iranian Studies*, 15:1/4 (1982), pp. 155–80.

WORKS IN FRENCH ABOUT EBRAHIM GOLESTAN

Esmaeelpour, Farid. *La genèse du cinéma d'auteur iranien: Ebrahim Golestan*. Paris: Éditions L'Harmattan, 2017.

Haghighat, Mamad. *Histoire du cinéma iranien, 1900–1999*. Paris: Cinéma du réel, Bibliothèque publique d'information, Centre Georges Pompidou, 1999.

Loppinot, Stéfani de. "Le choc des titans: un feu, Ebrahim Golestan." *Cinéma: revue semestrielle d'esthéthique et d'histoire du cinéma*, 7 (Printemps 2004), pp. 67–72.

PERSIAN ARTICLES TRANSLATED INTO ENGLISH

FOR A LIST OF THESE AND OTHER TITLES IN PERSIAN, SEE PP. 145–63)

Abd Elaheian, H. "A History of Hemingway's Works in Persian Literature." *Journal of Language and Literature*, 36:2 (2003), pp. 65–73.

Farhad, Tahmasebi, and Daniyali Marziyeh. "Reflecting on Rhetorical Aspects of Ebrahim Golestan's Musical Prose." *Studies of Literary Criticism*, 16 (Fall 2009), pp. 55–76.

Gholamali, Assadollah, and Ali Sheikhmehdi. "Dialogism in the Movie of the Brick and Mirror (Khesht va Ayeneh) (1965) by Ebrahim Golestan." *honar-ha ye ziba: honar-ha ye-namayeshi va musighi*, 22:2 (September 23, 2017), pp. 137–45.

Leila, Sadeghi. "Macrofiction as a New Sub-Genre in Ebrahim Golestan's Shekar-e Sayeh." *Literary Criticism*, 6:21 (Spring 2013), pp. 137–62.

———. "Textual Schema in the Formation of a New Version of 'Novel-in-Stories' Using a Cognitive Poetic Approach (Analyzing a Work by Ebrahim Golestan)." *New Literary Studies*, 46:4 (Winter 2014), pp. 87–109.

Noorian, S. Mehdi, and Shabnam Hatampour. "Oil Industry and Its Relation with the Works of Three Iranian Writers from the South of the Country (Ahmad Mahmood, Sadegh Choobak & Ebrahim Golestan." *Journal of Kavoshnameh in Persian Language and Literature*, 15:28 (September 23, 2014), pp. 209–39.

Poushaneh, Atena, and Morteza Babak Moien. "The Representation of Social Actors via Socio- Semantic Features in One Story by Ebrahim Golestan: A CDA Study." *Language Related Research*, 4:2 (July 10, 2013), pp. 1–25.

Saeid, Bozorg Bigdeli, Taheri Ghodratollah, and Mousivand Zahra. "On the Reflection of the 1953 Iranian Coup d'État in Ebrahim Golestan's Fictions." *Literary Text Research*, 15:50 (Winter 2012), pp. 81–106.

Shahidani, Shahab, and Parvin Rostami. "Reflection of Social Protest in the Films of the 1970s (Case Study: Secrets of the Jenny Valley Treasure (1973), Tangsir (1974), Rock Trip (1976))." *Journal of Historical Sociology* 11:2. (Winter 2020), pp. 175–202.

Tayefi, S.H. Tayefi, and A.R. Pourshabanan."Ibrahim Golestan, Founder of a New Prose." Journal of Stylistic of Persian Poem and Prose, 3:28 (January 1, 2010), pp. 109–30.

EBRAHIM GOLESTAN
BIBLIOGRAPHY IN PERSIAN
PAGES 145–164 FROM LEFT TO RIGHT

فهرست کتاب‌های ابراهیم گلستان

گلستان، ابراهیم. (۱۳۲۷). آذر ماه آخر پاییز. چاپ اول. تهران: نشر نقش جهان.

ـــــــ. (۱۳۳۴). شکار سایه: چند داستان. چاپ اول. تهران: نشر میهن.

ـــــــ. (۱۳۴۶). جوی و دیوار و تشنه. چاپ اول. تهران: نشر میهن.

ـــــــ. (۱۳۴۸). مَد و مِه. چاپ سوم. تهران: نشر صفا.

ـــــــ. (۱۳۵۳). اسرار گنج درّه جنی. چاپ اول. تهران: نشر آگاه.

ـــــــ. (۱۳۷۷). گفته‌ها. چاپ اول. لندن: نشر ویدا.

ـــــــ. (۱۳۷۴). خروس. چاپ اول. لندن: انتشارات روزن.

ـــــــ. (۱۳۸۳). نامه به سیمین. به کوشش دکتر عبّاس میلانی. تهران: نشر اختران.

ـــــــ. (۱۴۰۰). برخوردها در زمانهٔ برخورد. چاپ اول. تهران: انتشارات
بازتاب‌نگار.

ـــــــ. (۱۴۰۱). مختار در روزگار. چاپ اول. تهران: انتشارات بازتاب‌نگار.

فهرست ترجمه‌های ابراهیم گلستان

استالین، ژوزف. (۱۳۲۳). دیالکتیک. ترجمهٔ ابراهیم گلستان. چاپ شده به شکل
جزوه.

لنین، ولادیمیر. (۱۳۲۳). اصول مارکسیسم. ترجمهٔ ابراهیم گلستان. چاپ شده به شکل
جزوه.

همینگوی، ارنست. (۱۳۲۸). زندگی خوش کوتاه فرنسیس مکومبر. ترجمهٔ ابراهیم
گلستان. چاپ اول. تهران: انتشارات امیرکبیر.

تواین، مارک. (۱۳۳۳). ترجمهٔ ابراهیم گلستان. تهران: انتشارات روزن.

لندن، جک و دیگران. (۱۳۳۴). کشتی شکسته‌ها. ترجمهٔ ابراهیم گلستان. چاپ اوّل.
تهران: انتشارات صفی علیشاه با همکاری مؤسسهٔ انتشارات فرانکلین.

بودنهایم، ماکسول. (۱۳۳۵). «مرگ». ترجمهٔ ابراهیم گلستان. جُنگ هنر و ادب امروز،
دفتر دوّم (بهار)، صص. ۱۳۰-۱۳۱.

فلوبر، گوستاو. (۱۳۳۷). «از نامه‌های فلوبر». ترجمهٔ ابراهیم گلستان. ماهنامهٔ صدف
(شهریور)، صص. ۷۹۶-۸۰۲.

خیمه‌نز، خوان رامون. (۱۳۴۷). «مرغانی که می‌دانم». ترجمهٔ ابراهیم گلستان. دفترهای
روزن، شماره یک (زمستان)، صص. ۶۶-۶۷.

Compiled by Ameneh Yousefi

گوئلین، خورگه. (۱۳۴۷). «مرگ، دورادور». ترجمهٔ ابراهیم گلستان. دفترهای روزن، شمارهٔ ۳ (زمستان)، ص. ۶۹.

برناردشاو، جرج. (۱۳۵۴) دون ژوان در جهنم. ترجمهٔ ابراهیم گلستان. تهران: انتشارات آگاه.

فهرست مقالات، یادداشت‌ها، و گفتگوهای ابراهیم گلستان

گلستان، ابراهیم. (۱۳۲۵). «اتم و سیاست اتمی». ماهنامهٔ مردم.

———. (۱۳۴۳). «گفتگو با ابراهیم گلستان». کیهان اینترنشنال. شماره سوم.

———. (۱۳۴۸). «قیصر، سرمشق کاملی از مسعود کیمیائی برای مسعود کیمیائی». روزنامهٔ آیندگان.

———. (۱۳۶۹). «سی سال و بیشتر با مهدی اخوان». ایران‌شناسی، سال ۸، صص. ۷۵۵-۷۷۳.

———. (۱۳۷۲). «بیست و هشت پنج سی‌ودو». کلک، شمارهٔ ۴۱، صص. ۴۶-۵۱.

———. (۱۳۷۸). «به یاد دکتر اپریم اسحق در سالگرد درگذشت او». بخارا، شماره ۸ (مهر)، صص. ۳۱-۳۲۰.

———. (۱۳۸۴). «پایان این نماد نیکی کم همتا». بخارا، شمارهٔ ۴۲ (خرداد و تیر)، صص. ۳۶۴-۳۶۶.

———. (۱۳۸۴). «تقصیر را از که می‌بینی؟». سالنامهٔ شرق، شمارهٔ ۲، صص. ۴۸-۵۰.

———. (۱۳۸۴). «با محمد بهمن بیگی و لحظه‌های شرافت نورانی». نگاه نو، شمارهٔ ۶۸، ص. ۵۷.

———. (۱۳۸۶). «نامه ابراهیم گلستان به احمدرضا احمدی». گوهران، شمارهٔ ۱۶، صص. ۱۹۰-۱۹۴.

———. (۱۳۸۸). "یادنامه همایون صنعتی زاده (همایون صنعتی و حزب توده و شاه و گل سرخ)". مجله بخارا، شماره ۷۲ و ۷۳ (از ۴۲۹ تا۴۵۲).

———. (۱۳۸۸). «همایون = تک». بخارا، شمارهٔ ۷۲ و ۷۳ (مهر – دی ۱۳۸۸)، صص. ۴۲۹-۴۵۹.

———. (۱۳۹۰). «دیداری از گوشه‌های رشد در روزگار دگرگونی». فراسو، شمارهٔ ۱۴.

ـــــــ. (۱۳۹۱). «ابراهیم گلستان از شکار سایه‌ها می‌گوید». مهرنامه، صص. ۱۱۲-۱۱۴.

ـــــــ. (۱۳۹۲). «حزنی غرنده در زبانی پاک». در: همراه آن لحظه‌های گریزان: مقالات دربارهٔ زندگی و آثار مهدی اخوان ثالث. تهران: انتشارات زمستان.

ـــــــ. (۱۳۹۳). «طفلک طبری». مهرنامه، شمارهٔ ۳۷، ص. ۱۹۸.

ـــــــ. (۱۳۹۳). «لطفاً ما یکی را اول کنید که نیستیم و نخواستیم (نامهٔ ابراهیم گلستان به دبیر جشنواره فیلم تورنتو)». روزنامه اعتماد، شماره ۳۱۴۱ (۸ دی)، ص. ۱۲.

ـــــــ. (۱۳۹۴). «رشد یک نوسال طی تقدیر یک محیط». ماهنامهٔ تجربه، شمارهٔ ۱۰.

ـــــــ. (۱۳۹۴). «باید به فکر خود تعهد داشت: گفت‌وگو با ابراهیم گلستان به مناسبت تجدید چاپ سه کتاب گفته‌ها، کشتی شکسته‌ها و هکلبری‌فین». روزنامهٔ شرق، شمارهٔ ۲۳۴۶ (۲۲ تیر)، ص. ۱۰.

ـــــــ. (۱۳۹۴). «کیمیایی برایم تراژدی است: روایت ابراهیم گلستان ازآدم‌ها و قصه‌ها». روزنامه شرق، ۲۳۴۶ (۲۲ تیر)، ص. ۱۰.

ـــــــ. (۱۳۹۴). «روایت ابراهیم گلستان از مجادله با چپ گرایی (در گفتگو با مهدی یزدانی خرم)». مهرنامه، شمارهٔ ۴۴، صص. ۲۰۷-۲۱۲.

ـــــــ. (۱۳۹۴). «همیشه علیه چپ نوشتن فحش خوردن دارد». مهرنامه، شمارهٔ ۴۴، صص. ۲۰۷-۲۱۲.

ـــــــ. (۱۳۹۵). «آنجوری که کوک شده بود». بخارا، شمارهٔ ۱۱۵ (آذر - دی)، صص. ۴۷۲-۴۷۷.

ـــــــ. (۱۳۹۵). «در میان موج‌های زمانه». بخارا، شمارهٔ ۱۱۴ (مهر - آبان)، صص. ۳۵۰-۳۵۲.

ـــــــ. (۱۳۹۵). «من اهل تعزیه نیستم». ماهنامهٔ فیلم، شمارهٔ ۵۱۳، ص. ۱۵.

ـــــــ. (۱۳۹۵). «حرف ملکی کار خود را کرد: روایت ابراهیم گلستان از خلیل ملکی و سفرش به انگلستان». روزنامهٔ شرق، شمارهٔ ۲۷۰۶ (۲۷ مهر). ص. ۱.

ـــــــ. (۱۳۹۵). «در مرگ مردی که خواهان پاک گویی به پاک خواهی بود». روزنامهٔ شرق، شمارهٔ ۲۵۵۶ (۲۳ فروردین)، ص. ۹.

ـــــــ. (۱۳۹۵). «نظر ابراهیم گلستان دربارهٔ قاسم هاشمی‌نژاد». روزنامهٔ اعتماد، شمارهٔ ۳۴۹۴ (۱۶ مرداد)، ص. ۱۲.

ـــــــ. (۱۳۹۵). «در حضور شکسپیر: چهارصد سال شکسپیر و مقاله‌ای از ابراهیم گلستان». روزنامهٔ شرق، شمارهٔ ۲۷۷۸ (۲۷ دی)، ص. ۱۰.

ـــــــ. (۱۳۹۶). "نامه ابراهیم گلستان به پرویز جاهد دررابطه با بهرام بیضایی." روزنامه شرق .

ـــــــ. (۱۳۹۶). «ابراهیم گلستان از بیضایی می گوید». روزنامهٔ شرق، شمارهٔ ۲۹۳۸ (۲۵ مرداد ۱۳۹۶)، ص. ۱۴.

ـــــــ. (۱۳۹۶). «حرف زدن مکافات دارد: گفت‌وگوی احمد غلامی با ابراهیم گلستان». روزنامهٔ شرق، شمارهٔ ۳۱۰۶ (۱۴ اسفند)، ص. ۱۴.

ـــــــ. (۱۳۹۶). «یادداشت ابراهیم گلستان درباره صادق هدایت». هفته‌نامهٔ صدا.

ـــــــ. (۱۳۹۶). «روایت گلستان از کاوه: گفت‌وگوی عبّاس میلانی با ابراهیم گلستان دربارهٔ کاوه». فصلنامهٔ نیلوفر آبی، شمارهٔ ۳ (بهمن و اسفند)، صص. ۲۲-۲۵.

ـــــــ. (۱۳۹۷). «این است واقعیّت». بخارا، شمارهٔ ۱۲۵ (شهریور)، صص. ۱۵۹-۱۶۴.

ـــــــ. (۱۳۹۷). «قیصر ننه من غریم بازی روزگار نبود». روزنامهٔ اعتماد، شمارهٔ ۴۱۴۷ (۸ مرداد)، ص. ۸.

ـــــــ. (۱۳۹۷). «قیصر تحسین لمپنی نبود». روزنامهٔ شرق، شمارهٔ ۳۲۱۹ (۲۲ مرداد)، ص. ۱.

ـــــــ. (۱۳۹۷). «ابراهیم گلستان در نامه‌ای به شرق نوشت مسیو ابراهیم و ... ربطی به من ندارد». روزنامهٔ شرق، شمارهٔ ۳۳۴۶ (۲۹ دی)، ص. ۱۶.

ـــــــ. (۱۳۹۸). «سینایی و گلستان از محمّد ابراهیم جعفری می‌گویند». روزنامهٔ اعتماد، شمارهٔ ۴۳۴۱ (۲۴ فروردین)، ص. ۹.

ـــــــ. (۱۳۹۸). «سینایی و گلستان از محمّد ابراهیم جعفری می‌گویند». روزنامهٔ اعتماد، شمارهٔ ۴۳۴۱ (۲۴ فروردین)، ص. ۹.

ـــــــ. (۱۳۹۸)."نامه ابراهیم گلستان به ماهور احمدی درباره مسعود کیمیایی. روزنامه شرق.

ـــــــ. (۱۳۹۹). «اندوه جاودانه: بازخوانی چلچراغ از ۲۸ مرداد و دادگاه دکتر مصدق»، هفته‌نامهٔ چلچراغ، شمارهٔ ۷۸۶ (۲۵ مرداد)، ص. ۱۰-۱۵.

ـــــــ. (۱۳۹۹). «تمجید از فیلم‌های کیارستمی: نامه‌ای از ابراهیم گلستان». روزنامهٔ دنیای اقتصاد، شمارهٔ ۵۰۲۶ (۱۷ آبان)، ص. ۲۵.

ـــــــ. (۱۳۹۹). «نشریات روس‌ها در ایران: گفت‌وگوی علی دهباشی با ابراهیم گلستان)». مجلهٔ طبل، شمارهٔ ۳، صص. ۱۴۹-۱۵۸.

ـــــــ. (۱۳۹۹). «دربارهٔ پرویز ناتل خانلری». اندیشهٔ پویا، شمارهٔ ۶۸ (مرداد-شهریور).

ـــــــ. (۱۳۹۹). «گفت‌وگو با ابراهیم گلستان دربارهٔ نامه به سیمین: مانیفست گلستان»، روزنامهٔ شرق، شمارهٔ ۳۷۷۳ (۱ مرداد)، ص. ۶.

ـــــــ. (۱۴۰۰). «گپی با ابراهیم گلستان از صد سالگی، زمانهٔ برخورد و چیزهای دیگر». هفته‌نامهٔ چلچراغ، شمارهٔ ۸۴۱ (۲۰ آذر)، صص. ۱۰-۲۰.

ـــــــ. (۱۴۰۰). «بازرگان در آینهٔ پشت سر: گفت‌وگوی احمد غلامی با ابراهیم گلستان به مناسبت انتشار کتاب برخوردها در زمانهٔ برخورد». روزنامهٔ شرق، شمارهٔ ۴۲۰۳ (۴ بهمن)، ص. ۶.

فهرست کتاب‌های نوشته شده دربارهٔ ابراهیم گلستان

اسلامی، مجید. (۱۳۹۱). مفاهیم نقد فیلم، صص. ۲۳۶-۲۵۳. چاپ ششم. تهران: نشر نی.

امینی، احمد. (۱۳۷۰). صد فیلم. چاپ اول. تهران: نشر شیدا.

تهامی‌نژاد، محمد. (۱۳۸۰). سینمای ایران. چاپ دوم. تهران : نشر پژوهشهای فرهنگی.

ـــــــ. (۱۳۹۱). سینمای مستند ایران. چاپ دوم. تهران : انتشارات سروش.

جاهد، پرویز. (۱۳۸۴). نوشتن با دوربین: رودرو با ابراهیم گلستان. چاپ اول. تهران: نشر اختران.

حقوقی، محمد. (۱۳۷۷). مروری برتاریخ ادب و ادبیات امروز ایران. چاپ اول، تهران، نشر قطره.

سپانلو، محمدعلی. (۱۳۶۹). نویسندگان پیشرو ایران. چاپ سوم. تهران: انتشارات نگاه.

سیف، محسن، (۱۳۷۷). کارگردانان سینمای ایران: از اوگانیانس تا امروز. چاپ اول. تهران: انتشارات ایثارگران.

صالح پور، اردشیر. (۱۴۰۱). ادبیات نفتی. چاپ اول، تهران: نشر الیما.

صادقی، لیلا. (۱۳۹۲). نشانه‌شناسی و نقد ادبیات داستانی معاصر: مجموعه مقالات نقد و بررسی آثار ابراهیم گلستان و جلال‌آل‌احمد. تهران: انتشارات سخن.

ـــــــ. (۱۴۰۰). نقدادبی با رویکرد شناختی. چاپ اول، سه جلد، تهران: نشرلوگوس.

عسگری حسنکلو، عسگر. (۱۳۹۴). زمانه و آدم‌هایش.چاپ اول.چاپ اول. تهران:نشراختران.

فرهودی‌پور، فاطمه. (۱۳۹۵). کتاب‌شناسی نقد و بررسی ادبیات داستانی معاصر: دفتر دوم جلال آل احمد، صادق چوبک، سیمین دانشور، ابراهیم گلستان. زیرنظر حسن میرعابدینی. تهران: فرهنگستان زبان و ادب فارسی.

فیاد، حسن. (۱۳۹۴). از روزگار رفته: چهره به چهره با ابراهیم گلستان. چاپ دوم. تهران: نشرثالث.

مدرس صادقی، جعفر. (۱۴۰۰). سه استاد. چاپ اول. تهران: نشرمرکز.

میرصادقی، جمال. (۱۳۸۱). جهان داستان. چاپ اول،تهران: نشراشاره.

مهرابی، مسعود. (۱۳۸۲). تاریخ سینمای ایران از آغاز تا ۱۳۵۷. چاپ اول. تهران: انتشارات پیکان.

میر عابدینی، حسن. (۱۳۷۷). صد سال داستان نویسی ایران. چاپ اول. تهران: نشر چشمه.

ــــــــ. (۱۳۸۴). هشتاد سال داستان کوتاه ایرانی. چاپ اول. تهران: انتشارات خورشید.

هاشمی‌نژاد، قاسم. (۱۳۹۸). بوته بر بوته: آثار معاصران در بوتهٔ نقد. چاپ چهارم. تهران: انتشارات هرمس.

فهرست مقالات نوشته شده دربارهٔ ابراهیم گلستان

آتش پرور، حسین. (۱۳۹۰). «اغراق شگرد نو در روایت فیلم اسرار گنج دره جنی». نشریه نافه، شمارهٔ ۴۵، صص. ۱۱۲-۱۱۳.

آتش سودا، محمد علی. (۱۳۸۲). «گلستان سعدی و ابراهیم گلستان». مجله کتاب ماه ادبیات، شمارهٔ ۷۱، صص. ۵۴-۶۱.

ــــــــ. (۱۳۹۰). «تقابل نثر شاعرانه با زبان عامیانه در آثار ابراهیم گلستان». نشریه نافه، شمارهٔ ۴۵، صص. ۷۱-۶۸.

آزادگان، ژینوس (۱۳۷۵). «با باد صدای موج می‌آید». کلک، شمارهٔ ۷۶-۷۹ (تیر - مهر)، صص. ۷۹-۷۶.

آغداشلو، آیدین .(۱۳۶۷). «ابراهیم گلستان سینما». ماهنامه فیلم، شمارهٔ ۷۴.

احمدی، احمدرضا. (۱۳۸۶). «نامه احمدرضا احمدی به ابراهیم گلستان». مجله گوهران، شمارهٔ ۱۶، ص. ۱۸۹.

احسانی، وجیهه و رضویان، حسین. (۱۳۹۴). «کاربرد استعارهٔ دستوری گذرایی در مقایسهٔ سبک دو رمان: تحلیل تطبیقی سبک مدیر مدرسه و اسرار گنج درهٔ جنّی». مجله نقد ادبی، شمارهٔ ۲۹، صص.۱۴۳-۱۶۶.

اسحاقیان، جواد. (۱۳۸۸). «گزاره های مدرنیستی ابراهیم گلستان در داستان کوتاه به دزدی رفته ها». سال سوم . شماره یازدهم. ص ۲۲-۳۳.

ـــــــ. (۱۳۹۰). «بررسی سویه‌های مدرنیسم در جوی و دیوار و تشنه». نشریه نافه، شمارهٔ ۴۵. صص. ۹۷-۱۰۳.

اسلامی، مجید. (۱۳۸۶). «ترجمه همینگوی». ماهنامه فرهنگی هنری هفت، شمارهٔ ۳۷، ص. ۱۵.

اشرف ابیانه، شهرام. (۱۳۹۸). «عارفی که ناخواسته گذارش به کافهای شلوغ افتاده: سینماگران اصیل ایرانی، بخش پنجم: دنیای سینمایی ابراهیم گلستان». مجلهٔ سینما سینما (آنلاین): عارفی که ناخواسته گذارش به کافهای شلوغ افتاده/ سینماگران اصیل ایرانی بخش پنجم؛ دنیای سینمایی ابراهیم گلستان | پایگاه خبری تحلیلی سینما سینما (cinemacinema.ir)

اصغری، حسن. (۱۳۸۰). «همدم آرمانی: نقد داستان ماهی و جفتش از مجموعه داستان جوی و دیوار و تشنه». کلک، شمارهٔ ۱۲۵، صص. ۶۷-۶۸.

اکرمی، جمشید. (۱۳۹۱). «مردی که زیاد هم نمی‌دانست». ماهنامه فیلم، شمارهٔ ۲۳، صص. ۴۰-۴۵.

الوند، سیروس. (۱۳۸۲). «خشت اول خشت و آینه و سینمای اجتماعی ایران». نشریه دنیای تصویر، شمارهٔ ۱۱۷، صص، ۹۷-۹۶.

امامی، کریم. (۱۳۶۹). «چند خاطره با دریغ و درد». کلک، شمارهٔ ۶، صص. ۱۷۸-۱۸۲.

ایزدیار، محسن و غفاری، مهسا. (۱۳۹۰). «بررسی داستان سیاسنبو و خروس از منظر نقد ساختارگرایانه و مکتب اقلیمی جنوب». فصلنامهٔ زیبایی‌شناسی ادبی، سال ۲/ شمارهٔ ۸، ص شماره ۸ ، صص. ۱۲۱-۱۳۷.

بارسقیان، سرگه. (۱۴۰۰). «اسناد تازه‌یاب از سانسور کتاب ابراهیم گلستان اسرار ناگفته گنج دره جنّی». بخارا، شماره ۱۴۵ (مرداد - شهریور)، صص. ۳۲۸-۳۴۵.

بحرانی، اشکان. (۱۳۹۰). «گام معکوس گلستان میان کنش سینما و ادبیات داستانی در اسرار گنج دره جنی». نشریه نافه، شمارهٔ ۴۵، صص. ۱۱۴-۱۱۵.

بزرگ بیگدلی، سعید و موسیوند، زهرا. (۱۳۹۰). «بررسی بازتاب کودتای ۲۸ مرداد ۱۳۳۲ در آثار داستانی ابراهیم گلستان». مجلۀ متن‌پژوهی ادبی، شمارۀ ۵۰، صص. ۸۱-۱۰۶.

بهیان، شاپور. (۱۳۹۵). «اثر ادبی به منزله پاسخی ایدئولوژیک: بررسی جامعه شناختی آذر، ماه آخر پاییز». مجلۀ جامعه‌شناسی هنر و ادبیات، سال ۸/شمارۀ ۱، صص. ۱۳۵-۱۶۱.

بهار، شمیم. (۱۳۴۵). «دربارۀ یک تجربه‌ی سینمایی». مجلۀ اندیشه و هنر، کتاب ۵/ دفتر ۸ (اردیبهشت)، صص. ۱۰۹۲-۱۰۹۷.

بهبهانی، مرضیه. (۱۳۹۸). «بررسی ویژگی های سبکی در نثر داستانی ابراهیم گلستان». مجله مطالعات شهریارپژوهی، دوره ۵/شمارۀ ۲۱، صص. ۵۹-۸۰.

بهرام، پرویز. (۱۳۷۷). فروغ و سینما. تهران: نشر علم.

بیضایی، بهرام. (۱۳۴۱). «کارنامه فیلم گلستان». نشریۀ آرش، شمارۀ ۵، صص. ۵۱-۵۶.

بی‌نیاز، فتح الله. (۱۳۸۱). «نگاهی از دور: مروری بر آثار ابراهیم گلستان». روزنامۀ ایران (۲۱ آذر)، ص .

پاک‌طینت، وحید. (۱۳۸۶). «بعد از فروکش مد بعد از شکستن مه». نشریه شهر هشتم، شمارۀ ۶.

پوشنه، آته. (۱۳۹۰). «بینامتنیّت و ساخت داستانهای کلان در آذر ماه آخر پاییز». نشریه نافه، شمارۀ ۴۵، صص. ۸۲-۸۵.

بابک‌معین، مرتضی. (۱۳۹۲). «تحلیل گفتمان انتقادی در اثری از ابراهیم گلستان با استفاده از مؤلفه‌های جامعه شناختی- معنایی گفتمان مدار با توجه به بازنمایی کارگزاران اجتماعی». مجله جستارهای زبانی، شمارۀ ۱۴، صص. ۱-۲۶ .

پویان، منصور. (۱۳۹۰). «تپه های مارلیک مستندی شاعرانه». نشریه نافه، شمارۀ ۴۵، صص. ۸۹-۹۱.

تقی‌زاده، صفدر. (۱۳۹۰). «موج موج موج». نشریه هنگام، شمارۀ ۹۰.

تهامی‌نژاد، محمد. (۱۳۷۹). «سینما و افکار عمومی سازی در سال‌های ۱۳۱۶ تا ۱۳۲۷ (سال‌های فراموش شده سینما در ایران)» مجلۀ فارابی، شمارۀ ۳۹، صص. ۷۱-۱۴۰.

جاهد، پرویز. (۱۳۹۰). «همچون در یک آینه: بازخوانی خشت و آینه ابراهیم گلستان». نشریه نافه، شمارهٔ ۴۵، صص. ۹۶-۹۲.

جوانمردی، سارا و فارسیان، محمدرضا. (۱۳۹۲). «تحلیل محتوایی و ساختاری رمان آسوموار اثر امیل زولا و داستان مردی که افتاد نوشتهٔ ابراهیم گلستان». نقد زبان و ادبیات خارجی، سال ۶/شمارهٔ ۱، صص. ۷۳-۹۰.

چپردار، هادی. (۱۳۸۴). «چنین کنند با بزرگان». نشریهٔ هفت، شمارهٔ ۲۵، صص. ۶-۱۲.

خجسته، الناز، طایفی، شیرزاد. (۱۳۹۰). «نقد جامعه و فرهنگ در داستان از روزگار رفته حکایت». نشریه نافه، شمارهٔ ۴۵. صص. ۱۰۴-۱۰۷.

دانیالی، مرضیه. (۱۳۸۸). «آهنگهایی که نوشته شد نگاهی به نثر آهنگین در آثار ابراهیم گلستان». نشریه گلستانه: مجله فرهنگ و هنر، شمارهٔ ۱۰۲، صص. ۹۴-۹۶.

داریوش، هژیر. (۱۳۳۹). «نامه ای به مجله سینما». مجله سینما.

دستغیب، عبدالعلی. (۱۳۶۹). «داستان نویسی و داستان نویسان معاصر ایران (صادق هدایت، جلال آل احمد، سیمین دانشور، بهرام صادقی، ابراهیم گلستان)». کلک، شمارهٔ ۱، صص. ۲۷-۳۴.

ـــــ. (۱۳۷۶). «درونمایه قصه‌های گلستان». گزارش، شمارهٔ ۸۱، صص. ۳۹-۴۳.

دوایی، پرویز. (۱۳۴۴). «نقدی درباره خشت وآینه». بازنشر در گزارش فیلم، شمارهٔ ۹۷ (۱۳۷۶)، ص. ۸۶.

دهباشی، علی. (۱۳۹۹). «گفت‌وگوی علی دهباشی با ابراهیم گلستان دربارهٔنشریات روس‌ها در ایران». مجله طبل، شمارهٔ ۳، صص. ۱۴۹-۱۵۸.

رحیمان، بهزاد. (۱۳۶۷). «نقد فیلم اسرار گنج دره جنی». ماهنامه فیلم، شمارهٔ ۶۶.

رزنبام، جاناتان. (۱۳۸۶). «ابراهیم گلستان: شیر سینمای ایران». پتریکور (نشریه آنلاین): خشت و آینه: ابراهیم گلستان همراه نقدهایی از شمیم بهار، پرویز دوایی و احمد شاملو ـ مجله فرهنگی هنری پتریکور (pettrichor.com).

رستمی، پروین و شهیدانی، شهاب. (۱۳۹۸). «بازتاب اعتراض‌های اجتماعی در فیلم‌های دههٔ ۱۳۵۰ (مطالعهٔ موردی اسرار گنج درهٔ جنی، تنگسیر، سفر سنگ)». جامعه شناسی تاریخی، سال ۱۱/شمارهٔ ۲، صص. ۱۷۵-۲۰۲.

رضایی، مینا و حبیبی، سید محسن. (۱۳۹۲). «شهر، مدرنیته، سینما: کاوشی در آثار ابراهیم گلستان». هنرهای‌زیبا - معماری و شهرسازی، سال ۱۸/شمارهٔ ۲، صص. ۵-۱۶.

روانشادنیا، سمیه. (۱۳۹۸). «شهر تهران در آثار سینمایی دههٔ ۴۰ از منظر جامعه شناسی سینما با تأکید بر فیلم خشت و آینه». هویت شهر، شمارهٔ ۳۹، صص. ۷۹-۹۰.

زاهدی، محمد. (۱۳۸۶). «مختصری دربارهٔ کتاب نوشتن با دوربین به کوشش پرویز جاهد». چیستا، شمارهٔ ۲۴۴-۲۴۵، صص. ۴۰۷-۴۱۱.

زندی، ناهید. (۱۳۹۰). «ابراهیم گلستان و مکتب جنوب». نشریه نافه، شمارهٔ ۴۵، صص. ۱۱۹-۱۲۱.

سرسنگی، مجید و سلیمان‌زاده، حامد. (۱۳۹۸). «سینمایِ پیشرو ایران قبل از انقلاب اسلامی: فرخ غفاری، ابراهیم گلستان و فریدون رهنما». هنر و تمدن شرق، شمارهٔ ۲۵، صص. ۹-۱۴.

سیف ، محسن. (۱۳۵۷). «اسرار گنج دره جنی». ستارهٔ سینما، شمارهٔ ۲۴۷.

سیف الدینی، علی‌رضا. (۱۳۹۰). «نویسندگی ایرانی متن خواندنی ابراهیم گلستان ونسل سایه». نشریه نافه، شمارهٔ ۴۵، صص. ۶۶-۶۷.

سینا، محمد. (۱۳۸۵). «مروری بر چشم انداز سینمای مستند در ایران». فصلنامه سینمای فارابی، سال ۱۵/شمارهٔ ۳-۴. دوره ۱۵.

شاملو، احمد. (۱۳۶۷). «اسرار گنج دره جنی». ماهنامهٔ فیلم، شمارهٔ ۶۸.

شایان، سامان. (۱۳۸۲). «تاثیر گلستان بر ادبیات داستانی». نشریه بانی فیلم.

شهبا، محمد، طبرسا، محمد. (۱۳۹۰). «دلالت معنایی میزانسن در سینمای هنری ایران». هنرهای زیبا - هنرهای نمایشی و موسیقی، سال ۱۶/شمارهٔ ۲، صص. ۳۵-۴۶.

صابری، ایرج. (۱۳۵۳). «نقد اسرار گنج دره جنی». مجله رستاخیز جوان.

صادقی، بهرام. (۱۳۳۸). «در این شماره». مجله سخن.

صادقی، لیلا. (۱۳۸۹). «بررسی عناصر جهان متن بر اساس رویکرد بوطیقای شناختی در یوزپلنگانی که با من دویده‌اند». نقد ادبی، سال ۳/شمارهٔ ۱۰، صص. ۹۱-۱۱۳.

——. (۱۳۹۰). «حرکت یک هشتم کوه یخی بالای آب است: خوانش به دزدی رفته‌ها». نشریه نافه، شمارهٔ ۴۵، صص. ۷۴-۸۱.

ـــــــ. (۱۳۹۲). «داستان کلان به مثابه ژانری فرعی در شکار سایه ابراهیم گلستان». نقد ادبی، سال ۶/شمارهٔ ۲۱، صص. ۱۳۷-۱۶۲.

ـــــــ. (۱۳۹۲). «طرحوارههای متنی در ساخت شکل جدیدی از«رمان در داستان» با رویکرد شعرشناسی شناختی (تحلیل اثری از ابراهیم گلستان)». جستارهای نوین ادبی، شمارهٔ ۱۸۳، صص. ۸۷-۱۱۰.

صراف، غلامرضا. (۱۳۹۰). «داستان کوتاه امری ژرف ساختی است و نه روساختی». نشریه نافه، شمارهٔ ۴۵، صص. ۱۰۸-۱۱۱.

طالبی نژاد، احمد. (۱۳۷۷). «ما و غربال تاریخ: نامهای سرگشاده به ابراهیم گلستان». گزارش روز (۵ آذر).

طایفی، شیرزاد و پورشبانان، علی رضا. (۱۳۸۹). «ابراهیم گلستان پایهگذار نثری نوین». سبکشناسی نظم و نثر فارسی (بهار ادب)، سال ۳/شمارهٔ ۲، صص. ۱۰۹-۱۳۰.

طهماسبی، فرهاد و دانیالی، مرضیه. (۱۳۸۸). «تأمّلی بر وجوه بلاغی در نثر آهنگین ابراهیم گلستان». مطالعات نقد ادبی (پژوهش ادبی)، شمارهٔ ۱۶، صص. ۵۵-۷۵

عبداللهیان، حمید. (۱۳۸۳). «مضامین و اندیشه های مشترک در داستانهای جلال آل احمد و ابراهیم گلستان». پژوهشهای ادبی، شمارهٔ ۵، صص. ۱۱۷-۱۳۰.

عشقی، بهزاد. (۱۳۵۳). «نقد فیلم خشت و آینه». ماهنامه رودکی، شمارهٔ ۳۹-۴۰.

عقیقی، سعید. (۱۳۸۲). «موج انفجار جدایی خشت و آینه گذشته حال و آینده». دنیای تصویر، شماره ۱۱۷.

ـــــــ. (۱۳۹۰). «تجربه تصویرِ داستان داستانِ تصویر». ماهنامه تجربه، شماره ۵.

علینژاد، سیروس. (۱۳۹۱). «برخورد در زمان برخورد». هنگام، شمارهٔ ۸۷.

ـــــــ. (۱۳۹۱). «به قصه اعتقادی ندارم». سینما، شمارهٔ ۶۶۵.

غلامعلی، اسدالله و شیخمهدی، علی.(۱۳۹۶). «منطق مکالمه در فیلم خشت و آینه». هنرهای زیبا - هنرهای نمایشی و موسیقی، سال ۲۲/شمارهٔ ۲، صص. ۱۳۷-۱۴۵.

فرجامی، محمود. (۱۳۸۶). «چه کسی از ابراهیم گلستان نمیترسد؟ (نقدی بر گفتوگو با ابراهیم گلستان)». خردنامهٔ همشهری، شمارهٔ ۲۳، صص. ۴۲-۴۵.

فولادینسب، کاوه. (۱۳۹۰). «نگاهی به مقوله زبان در آثار داستانی ابراهیم گلستان نبض رالای انگشتان گرفتن و شناختن». نشریهٔ نافه، شمارهٔ ۴۵، صص. ۱۱۶-۱۱۸.

قاسمزاده، محمد. (۱۳۸۷). «گفتهها درباره نوشتهها». فتح، ص۳۱.

کاووسی، هوشنگ. (۱۳۸۵). «نامه به یک فیلم ساز واقعی». فصلنامه سینمایی فارابی، شمارهٔ ۵۹-۶۰.

کشاورز، مهدی. (۱۳۸۶). «سینمای مستند: نگاهی گذرا به تاریخ سینمای مستند ایران». مجله نقد سینما، شمارهٔ ۵۲، صص. ۳۲-۳۴.

کمالی سروستانی، مرضیه، موسوی، سید کاظم، صادقی، اسماعیل، و مرتضوی، سید جمال‌الدین. (۱۴۰۰). «بررسی و تحلیل بومی‌گرایی و ادبیات عامه در آثار ابراهیم گلستان». تفسیر و تحلیل متون زبان و ادبیات فارسی (دهخدا)، سال ۱۳/شمارهٔ پیاپی ۴۸، صص. ۲۵۱-۲۷۸.

کیوان، سپهر. (۱۳۸۲). «گمشده ای در غبار». قدس.

محمدی، صابر. (۱۳۹۰). «کدام فاعل شعر؟ کدام شاعرنثر؟». نشریه نافه، شمارهٔ ۴۵، صص. ۸۶-۸۸.

محمدی، مجید. (۱۳۷۰). «سینما و آینه (آینه از آندری تارکوفسکی یا خشت و آینه از ابراهیم‌گلستان)». فارابی، شمارهٔ ۱۱، صص. ۷۴-۸۱.

محمودی، حسن. (۱۳۸۴). «حکایتی از روزگار رفته». شرق.

مرادی، لیلا. (۱۳۸۶). «فرمالیسم در مجموعه آذر ماه آخر پاییز»، رودکی، شمارهٔ ۲۱.

مظاهری، رحمت. (۱۳۴۰). «نقدی درباره یک آتش». هنر سینما، شمارهٔ ۶.

معیریان، آرش. (۱۳۸۱). «گریز به شرایط ناهنجار جامعه (خشت و آینه ابراهیم گلستان)». نقد سینما، شماره ۳۴، صص. ۲۸-۳۰.

مولودی، فواد. (۱۳۹۶). «نقدی بر نخستین نمونهٔ روایتگری سوم شخص محدود در داستان فارسی(به دزدی رفته‌ها)». ادبیات پارسی معاصر، سال ۷/شمارهٔ ۲، صص. ۱۲۷-۱۴۷.

موناکو، جیمز. (۱۳۷۳). «آلن رنه اولین سالها (ترجمهٔ کامبیز کاهه)». نقد سینما، شمارهٔ ۴، صص. ۲۰۲-۲۰۵.

موسایی، بهزاد. (۱۳۸۰). «داستان‌های اقلیمی و داستان نویسان گیلان». ادبیات داستانی، شمارهٔ ۵۶، صص. ۱۸-۲۹.

میراحسان، احمد. (۱۳۹۲). "در تنهایی کاری کردن". نشریه هنگام. شماره ۹۲.

میلانی، عباس. (۱۳۸۱). «صیاد سایه ها». ایران‌شناسی، دوره جدید، سال ۴/شمارهٔ ۴-۵، صص. ۲۴۹-۲۷۸.

ناصری، ناصر، حسن زاده، شهریار، و وخشوری، کبری. (۱۳۹۸). «بررسی زبان زنانه و مردانه در داستان‌های ابراهیم گلستان و منیرو روانی‌پور از منظر جنسیت و رویکرد تعلیمی‌اخلاقی (مطالعۀ موردی: جوی و دیوار و تشنه و کولی کنار آتش)». پژوهشنامه ادبیات تعلیمی، شمارۀ ۴۴، صص. ۸۹–۱۱۷.

نورایی، جهانبخش. (۱۳۹۱). «فریاد و سکوت: خشت و آینه ابراهیم گلستان». ماهنامۀ صنعت سینما، شمارۀ ۱۲۲، صص. ۱۳۴–۱۳۶.

نوریان، سید مهدی و حاتم‌پور، شبنم. (۱۳۹۳). «نقش صنعت نفت در ظهور سه نویسندۀ صاحب سبک مکتب داستان‌نویسی جنوب (ابراهیم گلستان، صادق چوبک، احمد محمود)». کاوش‌نامۀ زبان و ادبیات فارسی، شمارۀ ۲۸، صص. ۲۰۹–۲۳۸.

ناصری، ناصر، حسن‌زاده، شهریار، و وخشوری، کبری. (۱۳۹۹). «مقایسۀ زبان زنانه و مردانه در داستان‌های ابراهیم گلستان و منیرو روانی‌پور از منظر زبان‌شناسی جنسیّت و جامعه‌شناسی (مطالعۀ موردی مدّ و مه و کنیز)». پژوهش‌های نقد ادبی و سبک شناسی، شمارۀ ۴۲، صص. ۱۷۱–۱۹۴.

فهرست پژوهش‌های دانشگاهی دربارۀ ابراهیم گلستان

آقایی، معصومه. (۱۳۹۲). بررسی تأثیرات متقابل عکاسی و ادبیات داستانی بر یکدیگر با نگاهی به داستان‌های کوتاه معاصر ایرانی با تأکید بر آثار ابراهیم گلستان و هوشنگ گلشیری. دانشگاه تهران، پایان‌نامۀ کارشناسی ارشد.

ابراهیمی، الهه. (۱۳۹۵). نقش روایت و زاویه دید در داستان‌های کوتاه ابراهیم گلستان. دانشگاه گیلان، پایان‌نامۀ کارشناسی ارشد.

احسانی، وجیهه. (۱۳۹۳). استعاره دستوری گذرایی به منزله شاخص تعیین سبک بر اساس دو اثر مدیر مدرسه و اسرار درّه‌ی جنّی. دانشگاه سمنان، پایان‌نامۀ کارشناسی ارشد.

ادریسی، محمد. (۱۳۹۶). بررسی کیفیت دو ترجمه از اثر هاکلبری فین بر اساس مدل جولیان هاوس. دانشگاه البرز، پایان‌نامۀ کارشناسی ارشد.

اسماعیلی، مسعود. (۱۳۹۸). تحلیل مؤلفه‌های مستند دهۀ ۴۰ و ۵۰ ایران بر اساس آرای بوردول در تعریف سینمای‌هنری (محمدرضا اصلانی، فریدون رهنما، خسرو سینایی، کامران شیردل، فروغ فرخزاد، پرویز کیمیاوی، ابراهیم گلستان). دانشگاه سوره، پایان‌نامۀ کارشناسی ارشد.

امینی، پرویز. (۱۳۹۷). بررسی بازتاب پایگاه و طبقه اجتماعی سینماگران موج نو ایران در آثار سینمایی آنان (ابراهیم گلستان، فرخ غفاری، کامران شیردل، و پرویز کیمیاوی). دانشگاه سوره، پایان‌نامهٔ کارشناسی ارشد.

بابایی، زهرا سادات. (۱۴۰۰). بررسی تأثیر آرای حزب توده بر سبک نوشتار نویسندگان برجسته دههٔ ۲۰ تا ۴۰ (بر اساس آثاری از جلال آل احمد، بزرگ علوی، ابراهیم گلستان، و محمود اعتمادزاده). دانشگاه ولی‌عصر رفسنجان، پایان‌نامهٔ کارشناسی ارشد.

باشی، مهوش. (۱۳۹۵). مقایسهٔ بومی‌گرایی در آثار غلامحسین ساعدی و ابراهیم گلستان. دانشگاه پیام نور فارس، پایان‌نامهٔ کارشناسی ارشد.

بنی‌فاطمی، ملیحه‌السادات. (۱۳۹۲). معماری نثر: بررسی تطبیقی کلیسای جامع ریموند کارور و جوی و دیوار و تشنه ابراهیم گلستان. دانشگاه گیلان، پایان‌نامهٔ کارشناسی ارشد.

بهاری،علیرضا. (۱۳۹۳). بررسی جامعه‌شناختی آثار ابراهیم گلستان. دانشگاه سیستان و بلوچستان، پایان‌نامهٔ کارشناسی ارشد.

پورمرادی، طیبه. (۱۳۹۰). تحلیل سبک‌شناختی آثار داستانی ابراهیم گلستان. دانشگاه مازندران، پایان‌نامهٔ کارشناسی ارشد.

جوانمردی، سارا. (۱۳۹۲). ناتورالیسم امیل زولا در مقابل ناتورالیسم ابراهیم گلستان با تکیه بر دو اثر آسوموار و مردی که افتاد. دانشگاه فردوسی مشهد، پایان‌نامهٔ کارشناسی ارشد.

حمیدی، زهرا. (۱۳۹۲).بررسی تطبیقی تاثیر نوآوری‌های ارنست همینگوی در زبان و عناصر روایی بر داستای های کوتاه ابراهیم گلستان. دانشگاه شهید چمران اهواز، پایان‌نامهٔ کارشناسی ارشد.

دانشور کیان، امیرحسین. (۱۳۹۸). مطالعهٔ تطبیقی گونه‌های زبانی در رمان ماجراهای هاکلبری فین در دو زبان فارسی و انگلیسی. دانشگاه شهید بهشتی، کارشناسی ارشد.

رحیمی علی‌آبادی، سمیه. (۱۳۹۲). بررسی مؤلفه‌های مدرنیسم در مجموعه داستان‌های کوتاه ابراهیم گلستان. دانشگاه مازندران، پایان‌نامهٔ کارشناسی ارشد.

سپهری، مهناز. (۱۳۸۸). بازنمایی مفهوم عقلانیت در ادبیات معاصر ایران با تکیه بر رمان (۱۳۳۰–۱۳۸۰). دانشگاه پیام نور تهران، پایان‌نامهٔ کارشناسی ارشد.

سهرابی ترکدره، صلاح‌الدین.(۱۳۹۵). شخصیت و شخصیت‌پردازی در آثار داستانی ابراهیم گلستان.دانشگاه زابل، پایان‌نامهٔ کارشناسی ارشد.

شاپسندزاده، آزاده. (۱۳۸۹). بررسی عناصر سینمایی در آثار داستانی ابراهیم گلستان. دانشگاه گیلان، پایان‌نامهٔ کارشناسی ارشد.

شاهینی،علی‌رضا.(۱۳۹۱).نقد و تحلیل درون‌مایه و شگردهای نقد ادبی نو در پنج اثر داستانی معاصر. دانشگاه اصفهان، پایان‌نامهٔ دکتری.

عبدالهی، ساقی. (۱۳۹۸). مقایسه ساختاری داستان‌های کوتاه جلال آل احمد با ابراهیم گلستان. دانشگاه پیام نور گیلان، پایان‌نامهٔ کارشناسی ارشد.

عسکری حسنکلو، عسگر. (۱۳۸۰). نقد و بررسی آثار داستانی ابراهیم گلستان. دانشگاه تربیت مدرس، پایان‌نامهٔ کارشناسی ارشد.

مرشدی میمندی، صدیقه. (۱۳۹۵). بررسی ادبیات اقلیمی در آثار داستان‌نویسان جنوب ایران. دانشگاه سمنان، پایان‌نامهٔ کارشناسی ارشد.

مساعد، مهری. (۱۳۸۹). بررسی نثر موزون در آثار داستان نویسان معاصر. دانشگاه یزد، پایان‌نامهٔ کارشناسی ارشد.

موسوی،فاطمه. (۱۳۹۲). هنجارگریزی زبانی در آثار داستانی ابراهیم گلستان. دانشگاه یاسوج، پایان‌نامهٔ کارشناسی ارشد.

موسوی، فاطمه. (۱۳۹۲). بررسی جامعه‌شناختی ادبیات داستانی سال‌های ۱۳۲۰ تا ۱۳۳۲ با تأکید بر داستان‌های دختر رعیت، زن زیادی، به دزدی رفته‌ها، حاجی‌آقا، نامه‌ها. دانشگاه سمنان، پایان‌نامهٔ کارشناسی ارشد.

موسوی‌زاده مبارکه، مهسا. (۱۳۹۷). بررسی تأثیر نفت بر ادبیات داستانی معاصر. دانشگاه یزد، پایان‌نامهٔ کارشناسی ارشد.

نیک‌رفعت، شادی. (۱۳۹۱). بررسی تکوین ساختار تولید سینمایی در ایران از ابتدا تا ۱۳۵۷ با استفاده از تئوری میدان پیر بوردیو. دانشگاه علم و فرهنگ تهران، پایان‌نامهٔ کارشناسی ارشد.

نیک سیر، زهره. (۱۳۹۷). تحلیل متون رئالیسم سوسیالیستی سال‌های ۱۳۳۲-۱۳۲۰ با رویکرد سبک شناسی انتقادی (ورق‌پاره‌های زندان، سگ ولگرد، بهار عمر، خیمه شب بازی، از رنجی که می بریم، شکنجه و امید، آذر ماه آخر پاییز، دختر رعیت). دانشگاه مازندران، پایان‌نامهٔ دکتری.

هداوند، حدیث. (۱۳۹۷). تحلیل سبک شناسانه و تطبیقی داستان های کوتاه ارنست همینگوی و ابراهیم گلستان. دانشگاه اراک، پایان‌نامهٔ کارشناسی ارشد.

یوسفی،آمنه. (۱۳۹۲). بررسی آثار داستانی ابراهیم گلستان با نگاهی به آثار سینمایی او از منظر ادبی و تاثیر متقابل آنها بر یکدیگر. دانشگاه همدان، پایان‌نامهٔ کارشناسی ارشد.

مطالب چاپ شده در روزنامه‌ها دربارۀ ابراهیم گلستان

«دیر زی آقای گلستان». روزنامه اعتماد، شمارۀ ۵۰۵۰ (۲۶ مهر ۱۴۰۰) ، ص. ۱۲.

«عذرخواهی ناشر از ابراهیم گلستان، حواشی مسیو ابراهیم و...». روزنامه شرق، شماره ۳۳۵۴ (۸ بهمن ۱۳۹۷)، ص. ۹.

«عذرخواهی مدیر نشر حکمت کلمه از ابراهیم گلستان». روزنامه دنیای اقتصاد، شماره ۴۵۳۳ (۷ بهمن ۱۳۹۷) ، ص. ۳۲.

«لیلی گلستان: پدرم بداخلاق، سلطه‌جو و زورگو بود!». روزنامه کیهان، شماره ۲۱۶۸۸ (۱۴ مرداد ۱۳۹۶)، ص. ۳.

«ترجمه دو نمایشنامه ایرانی در ایتالیا با مقدمه ابراهیم گلستان». روزنامه دنیای اقتصاد، شمارۀ ۴۰۰۰ (۱۶ اسفند ۱۳۹۵)، ص. ۳۲.

«مأموری که از کودتای ۲۸ مرداد بار خود را بست! / به بهانه مطالب سلسله‌وار درباره ابراهیم گلستان». روزنامه کیهان، شماره ۲۱۱۹۱ (۴ آبان ۱۳۹۴) ، ص. ۸.

«به بهانه سالروز تولد ۹۱ سالگی ابراهیم گلستان». روزنامهٔ اعتماد، شمارۀ ۲۸۰۶ (۲۸ مهر ۱۳۹۲)، ص. ۱۰.

«خط نگاره ابراهیم حقیقی در گالری گلستان». روزنامه ایران، شماره ۵۴۸۹ (۲۷ مهر ۱۳۹۲)، ص. ۲۴.

«در دفاع از کیمیایی ابراهیم گلستان فیلم‌هایش را به پاریسی‌ها نداد». روزنامه شرق، شماره ۳۰۳۳ (۲۲ آذر ۱۳۹۶)، ص. ۱۰.

«نشانه‌شناسی آثار ابراهیم گلستان در خانه هنرمندان». روزنامه شرق، شماره ۱۶۳۴ (۳ مهر ۱۳۹۱)، ص. ۲۰.

«حاشیه‌های نمایشگاه کتاب تهران در روزهای آخر ادامه دارد: ممنوعیت فروش کتاب خروس ابراهیم گلستان». روزنامه اعتماد، شمارۀ ۱۳۹۰ (۲۲ اردیبهشت ۱۳۸۶)، ص. ۲۰.

«ابراهیم گلستان: ۱۲ ماه پیش از روزی که مصدق نخست وزیر شد». روزنامه شرق، شماره ۳۶۷۶ (۴ فروردین ۱۳۹۹)، ص. ۴.

«حق با ابراهیم گلستان بود! به مناسبت نود و هفت سالگی ابراهیم گلستان». روزنامه شرق، شماره ۳۵۴۳ (۱۵ مهر ۱۳۹۸)، ص. ۱.

«نمایش فیلم ابراهیم گلستان در جشنواره ونیز». روزنامه دنیای اقتصاد، شماره ۴۳۷۸ (۲۸ تیر ۱۳۹۷)، ص. ۱۴.

«ژان لوک گدار و ابراهیم گلستان در یک قاب». روزنامه اعتماد، شماره ۴۱۱۲ (۲۸ خرداد ۱۳۹۷)، ص. ۱۵.

«چهره به چهره با ابراهیم گلستان». روزنامه شرق، شماره ۲۴۶۵ (۱۶ آذر ۱۳۹۴)، ص. ۱۱.

«سراغ ابراهیم گلستان نروید: توصیه های جمال میرصادقی درباره داستان خواندن و داستان نوشتن». روزنامه شرق، شماره ۱۱۰۶ (۱۶ آبان ۱۳۸۹) ، ص. ۲۰.

«تجلیل از ابراهیم گلستان: نامزدهای ۱۰ سال جایزه نویسندگان و منتقدان مطبوعات اعلام شد». روزنامه دنیای اقتصاد، شماره ۱۹۳۳ (۱۰ آبان ۱۳۸۸)، ص. ۳۰.

«ترجمه‌های ابراهیم گلستان همچنان در صف ارشاد». روزنامه آفتاب یزد، شماره ۲۲۳۸ (۱۹ آذر ۱۳۸۶)، ص. ۱۰.

«۲۶ مهر سالروز تولد ابراهیم گلستان است». روزنامه اعتماد، شماره ۴۴۹۱ (۲۵ مهر ۱۳۹۸)، ص. ۱۵.

«ابراهیم گلستان: رها شدن از شر مالاریا». روزنامه شرق، شماره ۳۱۰۱ (۱۴ اسفند ۱۳۹۶)، ص. ۱.

«قلعه انسانات ایرانی با مقدمه ابراهیم گلستان». روزنامه اعتماد، شماره ۳۸۰۵ (۲۳ اردیبهشت ۱۳۹۶)، ص. ۱۲.

«گفت وگو با ابراهیم گلستان در ماهنامه فیلم». روزنامه دنیای اقتصاد، شماره ۳۴۶۴ (۲ اردیبهشت ۱۳۹۴)، ص. ۳۲.

«ترجمه خلاقانه ابراهیم گلستان در کتاب کشتی شکسته‌ها». روزنامه اعتماد، شماره ۳۰۹۳ (۵ آبان ۱۳۹۳)، ص. ۱۶.

«تجربه با ابراهیم گلستان آمد». روزنامه شرق، شماره ۱۳۷۲ (۲۷ مهر ۱۳۹۰)، ص. ۲۰.

«کتاب تازه‌ای از ابراهیم گلستان». روزنامه دنیای اقتصاد، شماره ۱۰۸۸ (۷ آبان ۱۳۸۵)، ص. ۳۱.

«با صدهزار مردم تنهایی: درنگی بر حضور طبیعت شعر در قصه‌های ابراهیم گلستان به بهانه ۹۸ سالگی نویسنده». روزنامه اعتماد، شماره ۴۷۷۳ (۱ آبان ۱۳۹۹)، ص. ۱۱.

«هنرمند ذوالابعادی که باید از نو شناخت: به بهانه سالروز تولد ابراهیم گلستان». روزنامه اعتماد، شماره ۴۴۹۱ (۲۵ مهر ۱۳۹۸)، ص. ۱۱.

«ایستاده در فهم: برای ابراهیم گلستان». روزنامه اعتماد، شماره ۴۲۱۳ (۲۹ مهر ۱۳۹۷)، ص. ۱۶.

«تنش سنت و مدرنیته: گزارشی از نشست نشانه‌شناسی آثار نویسندگان نسل اول ایران: ابراهیم گلستان». روزنامه اعتماد، شماره ۲۵۱۳ (۱۷ مهر ۱۳۹۱)، ص. ۱۱.

«اول شخصِ دانای کل: ارتباط زاویه دید و لحن در داستان‌های ابراهیم گلستان». روزنامه شرق، شماره ۳۸۰۲ (۵ شهریور ۱۳۹۹)، ص. ۱۲.

«تصویر او، در ذهن من...: درباره مستند ابراهیم گلستان نقطه سر سطر». روزنامه اعتماد، شماره ۴۱۸۳ (۲۲ شهریور ۱۳۹۷)، ص. ۸.

«وقتی بچه، بچه بود: خوانشی از فیلم خشت و آینه ساخته‌ی ابراهیم گلستان». روزنامه اعتماد، شماره ۴۱۷۶ (۱۴ شهریور ۱۳۹۷)، ص. ۸.

«تیرانداختن به سوی سایه: سه روایت از در گذار روزگار اثر ابراهیم گلستان». روزنامه شرق، شماره ۲۶۶۴ (۳ شهریور ۱۳۹۵)، ص. ۹.

«آثار گلستان هنوز هم خواندنی است: در حاشیه انتشار مجدد آثار ابراهیم گلستان و استقبال چشمگیر از این آثار». روزنامه اعتماد، شماره ۱۱۳۳ (۲۱ خرداد ۱۳۸۵)، ص. ۵.

«پس زدن ناگهانی حریر خیال: داستان کوتاه ماهی و جفتش از ابراهیم گلستان (یک قرن داستان ایرانی)». روزنامه اعتماد، شمارۀ ۵۰۴۹ (۲۵ مهر ۱۴۰۰)، ص. ۷.

«مرد تنهایی‌های سوال‌مند برای زادروز ابراهیم گلستان». روزنامه اعتماد، شماره ۵۰۴۹ (۲۵ مهر ۱۴۰۰)، ص. ۷.

«حقیقت غریب‌تر از قصه ساخته: دو گزارش از ابراهیم گلستان در برخوردها در زمانه برخورد». روزنامه شرق، شماره ۴۱۱۷ (۲۱ مهر ۱۴۰۰)، ص. ۶.

«خشونت عقل: مد و مه ابراهیم گلستان و فرایندهای طرد». روزنامه شرق، شماره ۳۷۹۰ (۲۲ مرداد ۱۳۹۹)، ص. ۶.

«مردی که وطنش را با خود برد: ابراهیم گلستان، نامه به سیمین، و نقب زدن به اعماق». روزنامه شرق، شماره ۳۷۷۳ (۱ مرداد ۱۳۹۹)، ص. ۶.

«داستانی برای همیشه: کوتاه درباره ابراهیم گلستان به بهانه سالروز تولدش». روزنامه اعتماد، شماره ۴۴۸۷ (۲۱ مهر ۱۳۹۸)، ص. ۸.

«خروس از ابتدا راهنماست: نقدی بر کتاب خروس به مناسبت سالروز تولد ابراهیم گلستان». روزنامه اعتماد، شماره ۳۹۳۲ (۲۶ مهر ۱۳۹۶)، ص. ۱۲.

«صاحب مساحت باستانی هنر ایران: برای نود و دومین زادروز ابراهیم گلستان». روزنامه اعتماد، شماره ۳۰۸۱ (۲۰ مهر ۱۳۹۳)، ص. ۱۶.

«فروغ با گلستان به خوداکتشافی رسید: جایگاه شاعر فقید در تاریخ ادبیات معاصر در گفت و گو با اصغر ضرابی». روزنامه اعتماد، شماره ۵۱۵۲ (۲۸ بهمن ۱۴۰۰) ، ص. ۶.

«فیلم اسرار گنج دره جنی در قیاس با کتاب، موفق نیست: درباره اسرار گنج دره جنی ساخته ابراهیم گلستان». روزنامه شرق، شماره ۴۱۰۷ (۶ مهر ۱۴۰۰)، ص. ۶.

«رو در رو با تاریخ: یک کتاب، دو نویسنده: مد و مه ابراهیم گلستان به روایت احمد غلامی و احمد آرام». روزنامه شرق، شماره ۳۷۹۰ (۲۲ مرداد ۱۳۹۹)، ص. ۶.

«و ما بد نمی گفتیم به روشنفکران: تکه‌هایی از نامه ابراهیم گلستان به سیمین دانشور». روزنامه شرق، شماره ۳۵۴۳ (۱۵ مهر ۱۳۹۸)، ص. ۸.

«روشنفکر نسبتی با یاس و واخوردگی ندارد: روایت وتحلیلی متفاوت از ۲۸ مرداد ۱۳۳۲ در گفت وگوی اختصاصی با ابراهیم گلستان». روزنامه ایران، شماره ۶۲۸۹ (۲۸ مرداد ۱۳۹۵)، ص. ۱۲.

«نامگذاری تماشاخانه ایرانشهر به نام سمندریان، با پیام هایی از ابراهیم گلستان، سوسر تسلیمی و با حضور قالیباف صورت گرفت». روزنامه اعتماد، شماره ۲۱۸۶ (۱۰ اسفند ۱۳۸۸)، ص. ۱۶.

«مرور سینمای مستند ایران در فنلاند». روزنامه آفتاب یزد، شماره ۲۲۶۵ (۲۳ دی ۱۳۸۶)، ص. ۱۰.

«بازیگری جلوی دوربین را از ابراهیم گلستان آموختم: گفت‌وگو با جمشید مشایخی به مناسبت بازی در مجموعه تلویزیونی راز سکوت». روزنامه اعتماد، شماره ۱۴۶۱ (۱۶ مرداد ۱۳۸۶)، ص. ۱۰.

«وقتی موسیو ابراهیم دوباره سر زبان‌ها می‌افتد: اثری که که انتشار دیگر باره ترجمه اش بازتاب های فراوانی داشته است». روزنامه ایران، شماره ۶۹۸۵ (۷ بهمن ۱۳۹۷)، ص. ۸.

«شما می خواهید پز بدهم، پز نخواهم داد: به مناسبت نخستین نمایش خشت و آینه ساخته ابراهیم گلستان در جشنواره ونیز بعد از ۵۴ سال». روزنامه شرق، شماره ۳۲۳۷ (۱۵شهریور ۱۳۹۷)، ص. ۱۰.

«گلستان پنجره‌ای به روی شعر دنیا برای من گشود: گفتگو با احمدرضا احمدی». روزنامه ایران، شماره ۷۷۵۲ (۲۸ مهر ۱۴۰۰)، ص. ۱۶.

«فیلم گلستان در ردیف کلاسیک‌های تاریخ سینما: فیلم خشت و آینه در جشنواره ونیز به نمایش درمی‌آید». روزنامه ایران، شماره ۶۸۳۰ (۲۸ تیر ۱۳۹۷)، ص. ۲۲.

«روزگار مختار به روایت ابراهیم گلستان». روزنامه شرق، شماره ۴۲۹۵ (۱۶ خرداد ۱۴۰۱)، ص. ۱۱.

OTHER MAGE TITLES

History & Memoir

The Persian Sphinx:
Amir Abbas Hoveyda and the Iranian Revolution
Abbas Milani

Discovering Cyrus: The Persian Conqueror
Astride the Ancient World
Reza Zarghamee

The Artist and the Shah
Dust-Ali Khan Mo`ayyer al-Mamalek:
Memoirs of Life at the Persian Court
Edited, Translated, Introduced, and Annotated by
Manoutchehr M. Eskandari-Qajar

Tarikh-e Azodi, Life at the Court of the Early Qajar Shahs
Soltan Ahmad Mirza Azod al-Dowleh,
Edited and Translated Manoutchehr M. Eskandari-Qajar

Crowning Anguish: Taj al-Saltaneh
Memoirs of a Persian Princess
Introduction by Abbas Amanat / Translated by Anna Vanzan

Tales of Two Cities: A Persian Memoir
Abbas Milani

Lost Wisdom:
Rethinking Modernity in Iran
Abbas Milani

French Hats in Iran
Heydar Radjavi

Father Takes a Drink and Other Memories of Iran
Heydar Radjavi

The Persian Garden: Echoes of Paradise
Mehdi Khansari / M. R. Moghtader / Minouch Yavari

Closed Circuit History
Ardeshir Mohassess, foreword by Ramsey Clark

Mosaddegh: Ahead of Their Time
Nicolas Gorjestani

Persia Portrayed
D.T. Potts

Poetry

Faces of Love: Hafez and the Poets of Shiraz – Bilingual Edition
Translated by Dick Davis

The Mirror Of My Heart:
A Thousand Years of Persian Poetry by Women, Bilingual Edition
Translated by Dick Davis

Pearls That Soak My Dress: Elegies for a Child
Jahan Malek Khatun/ translated by Dick Davis

Layli and Majnun
Nezami Ganjavi / Translated by Dick Davis

Shahnameh: the Persian Book of Kings
Abolqasem Ferdowsi / Translated by Dick Davis

Rostam: Tales of Love and War from Persia's Book of Kings
Abolqasem Ferdowsi / Translated by Dick Davis

Borrowed Ware: Medieval Persian Epigrams
Introduced and Translated by Dick Davis

At Home and Far from Home
Poems on Iran and Persian Culture
Dick Davis

They Broke Down the Door: Poems
Fatemeh Shams / Introduction and translations by Dick Davis

The Layered Heart: Essays on Persian Poetry
In Celebration of Dick Davis
Edited by Ali-Asghar Seyyed Ghorab

Another Birth and Other Poems
By Forugh Farrokhzad, translated by Hasan Javadi and Susan Sallée
Bilingual edition

Obeyd-e Zakani: Ethics of Aristocrats and other Satirical Works
translated by Hasan Javadi

Milkvetch and Violets
Mohammad Reza Shafi'i-Kadkani/ translated by Mojdeh Bahar

Persia Observed Series

The Strangling of Persia:
A Story of European Diplomacy and Oriental Intrigue
Morgan Shuster

The Persian Revolution of 1905-1909
Edward Brown / Introduction by Abbas Amanat

In the Land of the Lion & Sun:
Experiences of Life in Persia from 1866-1881
C. J. Wills / Introduction by Abbas Amanat

A Man of Many Worlds:
The Diaries and Memoirs of Dr. Ghasem Ghani
Ghasem Ghani / Edited by Cyrus Ghani

Fiction

My Uncle Napoleon
Iraj Pezeshkzad / Translated by Dick Davis

Savushun: A Novel about Modern Iran
Simin Daneshvar / Translated by M.R. Ghanoonparvar

Daneshvar's Playhouse: A Collection of Stories
Simin Daneshvar / Translated by Maryam Mafi

Sutra and Other Stories
Simin Daneshvar / Translated by Hasan Javadi & Amin Neshati

Stories from Iran: A Chicago Anthology 1921-1991
Edited by Heshmat Moayyad

Garden of the Brave in War
Terence O'Donnell

King of the Benighted
Houshang Golshiri / Translated by Abbas Milani

Black Parrot, Green Crow: A Collection of Short Fiction
Houshang Golshiri / Translated by Heshmat Moayyad et al.

Seven Shades of Memory: Stories of Old Iran
Terence O'Donnell

Cookbooks

*Food of Life: Ancient Persian and
Modern Iranian Cooking and Ceremonies*
Najmieh Batmanglij

Joon: Persian Cooking Made Simple
Najmieh Batmanglij

Cooking in Iran: Regional Recipes and Kitchen Secrets
Najmieh Batmanglij

Silk Road Cooking: A Vegetarian Journey
Najmieh Batmanglij

From Persia to Napa: Wine at the Persian Table
Najmieh Batmanglij, Dick Davis, Burke Owens

A Taste of Persia: An Introduction to Persian Cooking
Najmieh Batmanglij

Cinema

The Films of Makhmalbaf: Cinema, Politics, and Culture in Iran
Eric Egan

Masters & Masterpieces of Iranian Cinema
Hamid Dabashi

My Favorite Films
Cyrus Ghani

Willem Floor Books

Persian Gulf Series

A Political and Economic History of 5 Port Cities, 1500–1750

*The Rise of the Gulf Arabs, The Politics of Trade on the Persian Littoral,
1747–1792*

The Rise and Fall of Bandar-e Lengeh, The Distribution Center for the Arabian Coast, 1750–1930

Bandar Abbas: The Natural Trade Gateway of Southeast Iran

Links with the Hinterland: Bushehr, Borazjan, Kazerun, Banu Ka'b, & Bandar Abbas

The Hula Arabs of The Shibkuh Coast of Iran

Dutch-Omani Relations: A Political History, 1651–1806

Muscat: City, Society and Trade

Karkh: The Island's Untold Story (with D.T. Potts)

The Persian Gulf: Bushehr: City, Society, & Trade, 1797-1947

The Rebel Bandits of Tangestan

Iranian History Series

Agriculture in Qajar Iran

Public Health in Qajar Iran

The History of Theater in Iran

A Social History of Sexual Relations in Iran

Guilds, Merchants, and Ulama in Nineteenth-Century Iran

Labor & Industry in Iran 1850 -1941

The Rise and Fall of Nader Shah: Dutch East India Company Reports 1730-1747

Games Persians Play: A History of Games and Pastimes in Iran from Hide-and-Seek to Hunting

History of Bread in Iran

Studies in the History of Medicine in Iran

Salar al-Dowleh: A Delusional Prince and Wannabe Shah

Kermanshah: City and Province, 1800-1945

History of Hospitals in Iran, 550–1950

The Beginnings of Modern Medicine in Iran

Food Security in Iran: Edareh-ye Arzaq, 1910–1935

Annotated Translations

German Sources on Safavid Persia
Exotic Attractions in Persia, 1684–1688: Travels & Observations
Engelbert Kaempfer

A Man of Two Worlds: Pedros Bedik in Iran, 1670–1675
translated with Colette Ouahes from the Latin
Astrakhan Anno 1770
Samuel Gottlieb Gmelin
Travels Through Northern Persia 1770–1774
Samuel Gottlieb Gmelin

Titles and Emoluments in Safavid Iran: A Third Manual of Safavid
Administration
Mirza Naqi Nasiri

Persia: An Area Study, 1633
Joannes de Laet
translated with Colette Ouahes from the Latin

WILLEM FLOOR IN COLLABORATION WITH HASAN JAVADI

Persian Pleasures
How Iranians Relaxed Through the Centuries
with Food, Drink and Drugs

Awake: A Moslem Woman's Rare Memoir of Her Life
and Partnership with the Editor of Molla Nasreddin,
the Most Influential Satirical Journal of the Caucasus and Iran,
1907–1931

The Heavenly Rose-Garden: A History of Shirvan & Daghestan
Abbas Qoli Aqa Bakikhanov

Travels in Iran and the Caucasus, 1652 and 1655
Evliya Chelebi

Audio Books

Faces of Love: Hafez and the Poets of Shiraz
Translated by Dick Davis / Penguin Audio / Read by
Dick Davis, Tala Ashe and Ramiz Monsef

The Mirror of My Heart:
A Thousand Years of Persian Poetry by Women
Translated by Dick Davis / Penguin Audio / Read by
Dick Davis, Mozhan Marno, Tala Ashe and Serena Manteghi

Layli and Majnun
Nezami Ganjavi / Translated by Dick Davis
Penguin Audio / Read by
Dick Davis, Peter Ganim, Serena Manteghi and Sean Rohani

Vis and Ramin
Fakhraddin Gorgani / Translated by Dick Davis
Mage Audio / Read by
Mary Sarah Agliotta, Dick Davis (introduction)

My Uncle Napoleon
Iraj Pezeshkzad / Translated by Dick Davis
Mage Audio / Read by
Moti Margolin, Dick Davis (Introduction)

Savushun: A Novel about Modern Iran
Simin Daneshvar / Translated by M.R. Ghanoonparvar
Mage Audio / Read by
Mary Sarah Agliotta, Brian Spooner (Introduction)

Crowning Anguish: Taj al-Saltaneh
Memoirs of a Persian Princess
from the Harem to Modernity, 1884–1914
Introduction by Abbas Amanat / Translated by Anna Vanzan
Mage Audio / Read by
Kathreen Khavari

www.ingramcontent.com/pod-product-compliance
Lightning Source LLC
Chambersburg PA
CBHW070411100426
42812CB00005B/1713